HOW TO DETECT DAMAGED, ALTERED,

AND REPAIRED STAMPS

PAUL W. SCHMID

Published by

**krause
publications**

700 E. State Street • Iola, WI 54990-0001
Telephone: 715/445-2214

Please call or write for our free catalog.
Our toll-free number to place an order or obtain a free catalog is 800-258-0929
or please use our regular business telephone 715-445-2214
for editorial comment and further information.

Library of Congress Catalog Number: 96-77478
ISBN: 0-87341-454-3

Printed in the United States of America

to my father

TABLE OF CONTENTS

PREFACE TO THE 1996 PRINTING

It is said, "The more things change, the more they stay the same." I certainly think this to be true with regard to the stamp market and the number of altered and repaired stamps that continue to appear. In the 17 years that have passed since this book's publication, the market for stamps has indeed changed.

The investors of the late 1970s and early 1980s quickly learned that even stamps offered considerable capital risks. Not only did one have to worry about quality, but it soon became apparent that most investors were not particularly interested in the long haul. As other, more traditional markets appeared to offer quicker and easier profits, large numbers of "investment grade" stamps flooded the market and precipitated the inevitable decrease in prices. Quickly, the stamp market was returned to the strong and secure hands of the collector, and it continues to be a collector-dominated market today.

What hasn't changed, however, is the prevalence of altered and repaired stamps that continue to plague the market. While the numbers may not be as great as they had been, the proportion seems to me to be about the same. This observation is not based on any special study through my part, but simply on the flow of material through various expert committees and across my desk.

Knowledge continues to be the collector's best ally. It is also what has always separated the true collector from the casual accumulator. If this book continues to provide readers with valuable information, then it has served its purpose. And for that I am pleased.

Paul W. Schmid
Huntington, New York
May 1996

PREFACE TO THE FIRST PRINTING

During the last few years the hobby has experienced a tremendous influx of new collectors and investors, which in turn has resulted in an unprecedented demand for scarce, high-quality stamps. As a result of this demand, some areas of the market have been flooded with bogus and repaired stamps, and their detection has become a major problem with concerned collectors and dealers. It is important for the dealer or collector to be able to evaluate a stamp's condition with reasonable certainty. Rarities, skillfully faked stamps, or those which are routinely confused with scarcer varieties may still require authentication by an expert; however, there are a great number of damaged, altered, and repaired stamps in the market that the interested dealer and collector can learn to detect.

Articles on various aspects of the subject have appeared from time to time in many different periodicals, bulletins, and journals; but appearing as they have, over a number of years and in many sources, they have not been readily accessible to the average individual.

This book is a compilation of information gathered and knowledge learned over many years of collecting and dealing in stamps. While much of it relates only to United States issues, there are those sections which are applicable to any stamp, and hopefully this will be of interest to all.

Paul W. Schmid
Huntington, New York
August 1979

ACKNOWLEDGMENTS

The following individuals provided needed assistance during the writing of this book and I gratefully acknowledge their help: Franklin Dillman, Richard Ehrlich, William Mesibov, Susan Sherman, and Roy White.

For the photography I would like to thank Carl Mamay.

I am especially appreciative for the cooperation extended to me by the Philatelic Foundation in New York.

And a special thanks to my wife, Lorraine, for her help from start to finish.

Other books by Paul Schmid:
The Expert's Book: A Practical Guide to the Authentication of United States Stamps. Washington/ Franklin Issues, 1908-1923. Palm Press, 7 High Street, Suite 300, Huntington, NY 11743.

Chapter One

DAMAGED AND REPAIRED STAMPS

Introduction

Rarity and demand notwithstanding, condition is the basis of a stamp's price. It is not uncommon for a stamp in choice condition to be valued many times more than an inferior copy of the same variety. Such wide price spreads have made it profitable to repair damaged stamps so that they appear to be sound copies. Stamp repair is not a new phenomenon, although very early repairs were probably done more for aesthetic reasons than for economic gain. As prices for choice material escalate, collectors and dealers are examining individual stamps more closely than ever before, and as a result, the repairers are becoming more proficient.

There are a great number of damaged, altered, and repaired stamps in the market today which can be detected by the knowledgeable amateur. This chapter and those that follow will teach the reader how to recognize such stamps.

Thins

A stamp which is missing some paper from its back, so that a particular area is thinner than the surrounding area, is called a thinned stamp. Such a defect is usually caused by mishandling, and often results from the improper removal of a hinge. Since the missing paper comes from the back of the stamp, a thin cannot usually be seen when the stamp's face side is viewed by reflected light.[1] A thin can be minute, perhaps less than the size of a pinhead, or extensive, affecting seventy-five percent or more of the total stamp area. A thin can be shallow, that is, one in which only the barest amount of paper has been removed, or it can be deep, one where much of the original paper thickness is missing. Thins are most prevalent in the area of a previous hinge, and this is true whether the stamp is unused or used.

The Detection of Thins

Sometimes an examiner will hold a stamp to the light, looking for an area that shows more translucency than the surrounding area. This is one way to check for an obvious thin, but not a very reliable method, since a small or shallow thin would probably not be noticeable. What may appear to be a thin may only be a watermark, and an unused stamp with a small amount of missing gum may appear to be thin, when in reality it is not.

A thin can be detected by placing a stamp face down in a black tray containing watermark fluid. This procedure, commonly referred to as "dipping," will reveal a thin as a dark patch. The deeper the thin, the darker it will appear in fluid. Further confirmation of a thin can usually be had by removing the stamp from the fluid, placing it face down on a clean blotter, and carefully observing the stamp as it slowly air dries. As the stamp paper begins to "white-up," that is, regain its opacity as the fluid dries, the thin spot will again be visible. It will now appear as a white patch for a brief second or two, the result of thinner paper and numerous broken paper fibers in the area of the thin drying more quickly than the surrounding paper. This is a procedure that many fail to take advantage of, yet it is extremely useful in detecting a number of easily

[1]If paper is missing from the face side of a stamp, the defect is called a surface scrape.

overlooked thins. A very shallow, small thin can be difficult to observe in fluid, as can one that exists in a watermark, since like a thin, a watermark also appears darker in fluid than the surrounding paper. A thin that occurs directly opposite a cancellation on a used stamp tends to be masked by the dark cancel. Thins in orange or yellow stamps can at times be difficult to detect in fluid because of the high contrast that results between the printed portion of the stamp and the black background of the watermark tray. Other gum disturbances, particularly those resulting from previous hinges, or the presence of a hinge remnant itself will sometimes cause whiting-up to take place even though there is no thin present. They will not, however, appear as dark patches when viewed in fluid. In many cases the cycle of dipping-observing-drying-observing must be repeated several times before it can be ascertained that a thin does or does not exist.

The Repair and Concealment of Thins

A thin is commonly repaired by filling it with a pulp-like mixture, allowing this mixture to dry, and then gently sanding the back of the stamp until the filled area is level with the rest of the surface. The repaired thin is often concealed by regumming. Therefore, even if a stamp has full, undisturbed gum, do not dismiss the possibility of finding a thin, unless it is certain that the gum is original.[2] The technique of observing a stamp dry after it has been dipped is not helpful in this instance, since the repair and the regumming effectively prevent any whiting-up from taking place. When held to a light, such a stamp will usually not appear to be thin. However upon dipping the stamp in watermark fluid, a lighter area will probably appear where the thin has been filled. Thickness, paper composition, and the adhesive used to bind the repair to the stamp all affect the final translucency in fluid, and repairing a thin so that it has the same appearance in fluid as the original paper is almost impossible. Examination of the stamp under ultraviolet light can also be helpful, as the repair may sometimes be revealed at

[2]Though uncommon, thins can exist in stamps with full original gum. The results of improperly manufactured paper, they are usually found only on early issues.

these wavelengths.

There are several ways to conceal rather than repair a thin. If the stamp is used, an additional cancellation can be placed opposite the thin, thus making its detection more difficult. Pieces of a hinge can also be used to conceal a thin, but they cannot usually mask a thin completely. After observing the stamp in watermark fluid, if a thin under a hinge remnant is suspected, the hinge should be removed. If the stamp is cancelled, simply soak it in water, carefully wash the hinge away, and allow the stamp to dry completely before returning to the examination. If a thin is suspected under a firmly adhered hinge on an unused stamp, follow the procedure for the removal of such a hinge as detailed in this book's chapter on gum. One should not conclude that any stamp with a hinge remnant has a thin, as the majority of such stamps do not. Such a stamp is simply one that requires more careful study.

Small thins of a suitable size and shape can sometimes be hidden by the addition of a fake watermark. Such a "watermark" can be applied by selectively thinning the stamp paper in the shape of the genuine watermark (fig. 1.1). Detection of this alteration in a

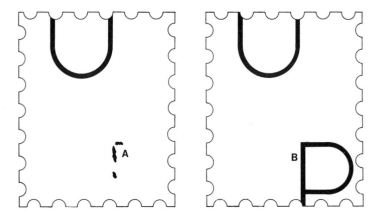

Figure 1.1. A Thin Altered to Resemble a Watermark. Thins of a suitable size and shape (A) can at times be hidden by the addition of a fake watermark (B). Knowledge of the genuine watermark layout is helpful in detecting this alteration.

4

used stamp is accomplished by watching the stamp dry after it has been dipped in watermark fluid. Thins will white-up, but legitimate watermarks will not. Unused stamps that have been regummed over such an alteration should be carefully examined to determine whether the watermark is the correct size and shape, and more importantly, whether it is in the correct position. Detailed layouts of single and double-line watermarks are available in the literature.[3]

Tears and Creases

While some tears or creases may be readily apparent, often these faults are difficult if not impossible to see without immersing the stamp in watermark fluid. In fluid, even a minute tear or a light crease will appear as a dark line. Differentiating between a crease and a repaired tear, however, is not always simple, and it is important that one be able to make this distinction.

In watermark fluid a tear will normally appear as a slightly jagged, dark line that starts at a stamp's edge and continues for some distance into the body of the stamp. A crease, however, will usually appear as a fairly straight line that begins at one edge of a stamp and continues to another edge. Often a crease will not appear as dark as a tear, and the less severe the crease, the lighter it will appear in fluid. An internal tear is one which is wholly confined to the body of the stamp; that is, one that does not reach to an edge. This type of tear, while fairly scarce, is most frequently encountered in grilled stamps, since the paper in the area of the grill is very fragile. Figure 1.2 is a schematic representation of a stamp which illustrates these various faults.

Removal of a crease usually starts with a prolonged soaking of the stamp in water, followed by the application of considerable pressure to the stamp while drying. It is likely that the crease will

[3]*Scott Specialized Catalogue of United States Stamps 1979* (New York, 1978), p. xviii.

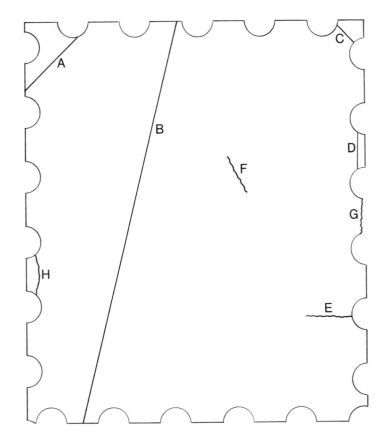

Figure 1.2. Schematic Representation of Common Stamp Faults. Major creases (A,B) and perforation creases (C,D) will usually appear in watermark fluid as straight lines which travel from edge to edge. A tear (E) will usually appear very dark in fluid and be slightly jagged. An internal tear (F) exists entirely within the body of the stamp. A short perforation (G) is often repaired by adding additional paper to the tip; however the joining line (H) usually appears jagged or slightly curved.

still be visible upon immersion of the stamp in watermark fluid, as a crease can almost never be removed completely, only lightened.

Internal tears and those which have not resulted in the stamp being torn into two or more pieces are routinely "closed" by gluing torn parts back together with an adhesive. Their detection can be difficult unless the stamp is placed in fluid, where they will show up as dark lines. Like thins, tears will white-up briefly if allowed to air dry slowly. If what is thought to be a tear affects the design portion of a stamp, it should be carefully examined from the face side as well. Under good magnification, sometimes a slight misregistration of the design at the site of the tear will be apparent. Such a detail is strong evidence that the stamp has been torn and not simply creased (fig. 1.3). The tear that separates a stamp into two or more pieces is more difficult to repair, but the method of detection is the same.

Figure 1.3. A Torn Stamp. The tiny tear starts directly below the letters "E" and "F" and is visible in watermark fluid as a dark line. Close examination of the face side reveals a slight misregistration of the design, thus confirming the fact that the stamp has been torn, and not simply creased.

Torn perforations are commonly encountered faults. All the perforation tips around a stamp should be approximately the same length. If any are significantly shorter, the quality of the stamp is lessened. Variously described as "nibbed," "blunt," "ragged," "short," "torn," or "missing" perforations, each term implies a greater or lesser degree of damage. These terms are subjective and their meanings will vary with each describer.

There are two ways to alter the appearance of a short or missing perforation tip. The first is to slightly shorten the tips of the adjoining perforations. This gives the damaged perforation tip the appearance of not being so short. Figure 1.4 shows a stamp before and after such an alteration.

The second type of alteration, one that is more serious, is a repair that adds to or replaces a short or missing per-

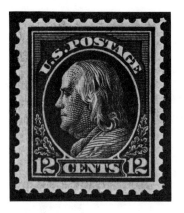 

Figure 1.4. Short Perforation, Before and After Alteration. Before alteration, the short perforation is clearly visible at the upper left. However, after the surrounding perforations were all slightly shortened, the damaged perforation does not appear to be so short. Note also that what may have looked like a short perforation at the bottom was in fact a perforation of acceptable length, only appearing short because of the extra long perforations surrounding it.

foration tip. When skillfully executed, this repair can be difficult to detect. It will, however, be visible when the stamp is placed in watermark fluid. Care must be taken not to mistake the added perforation for a creased perforation. The latter appears in fluid as a grayish, straight line, while the joining line of an added perforation will often appear dark and somewhat jagged (fig. 1.2). It is important to be able to differentiate between a creased perforation and an added perforation, as the latter is a more serious fault and has a greater effect on a stamp's value. Examination should also be made using ultraviolet light, as sometimes at these wavelengths the added perforation will appear different from the rest of the stamp.

Plate number blocks and other multiples are frequently encountered with separated perforations between the stamps or in the selvedge. Tears in the selvedge perforations of flat plate printed stamps were often the normal result of handling at the printer, and it is generally agreed that minimal selvedge separation in such plate blocks does not adversely affect the item's value.[4] Separation in rotary press printed plate blocks is more damaging. Early twentieth century and nineteenth century multiples normally exist with some separation in the selvedge or between the stamps themselves. Many sellers specifically mention this fact and state that such separation will not be grounds for an item's return.

Since the value of a plate block is lessened if there are a large number of separated perforations, attempts to rejoin these perforations are sometimes made. This repair can be accomplished using almost any glue or mucilage, but upon examination in watermark fluid, the rejoined separation will be visible as a dark line. Creased perforations can have a similar appearance, and often the only way to tell whether the perforations have been creased, or separated and rejoined, is by careful examination under good light with a strong magnifying glass. Look for any signs of glue used to rejoin the perforations, and examine the paper fibers to determine whether they

[4]The acceptable number of separated perforations per item can vary according to the item itself as well as with the individual buyer and seller. A total of a half-dozen or so separated perforations in the selvedge of a twentieth century, flat plate printed plate block is not considered detrimental by most collectors and dealers.

are continuous or broken. Examination under ultraviolet light can also be helpful, as sometimes the glue used to rejoin the perforations will be visible at these wavelengths.

Severely creased perforations can also affect the value of a multiple. A multiple should be stiff and not droop along one or more rows of perforations. If when placed in watermark fluid a multiple appears to be heavily creased along a particular row, yet it is stiff and fresh when dry, the chances are good that its perforations have been rejoined.

Other Faults

Pinholes

A pinhole is a tiny hole in a stamp, and while it is almost always of unknown origin, it is interesting to note that in the early days of the hobby, stamps were often pinned to display boards by sellers. A pinhole can easily be seen when a stamp is held to a bright light, and in fluid it appears as a tiny, black spot. When a pinhole appears in an otherwise flawless stamp, however, it can often go completely unnoticed.

A pinhole can be repaired by filling it with a pulp-like mixture and regumming over the repair. Such a repair will appear in watermark fluid as a tiny, light spot. Careful examination of the face side of the stamp at the site of the suspected pinhole will usually confirm any such repair.

Included Perforations

Sometimes called perforation inclusions, these flaws result from one or more of the tiny, circular pieces of paper produced during the perforating process inadvertently becoming a part of the finished stamp. Such inclusions exist in three distinct forms, which vary according to when and where the circular bit was incorporated into the manufacturing process:

> *1. On the back of the stamp, under the gum, having been pressed into the stamp during the printing process.*

> *2. On the face of the stamp, pressed into the paper during the printing process.*

> *3. On the face or gum side, pressed into the stamp after it was printed or gummed.*

The second inclusion is considered the most damaging, since it is possible for the small bit to come loose and leave a circular depression devoid of color on the face of the stamp. Attempts are usually made to remove an inclusion of the third type if it is on the face side, so as not to have a white spot appear on the printed portion of the stamp.

Inclusions can be detected by placing the stamp in watermark fluid. If the bit is still attached to the stamp, it will appear as a light, perfectly round spot. If the bit has been removed or fallen off, the circular spot will appear darker than the surrounding paper. These defects are often described as "tiny, natural perforation inclusions," and while the statement is perfectly correct, it tends to minimize the actual damage that can be present.

Paper Specks

The paper speck, like the perforation inclusion, is another defect that occurs naturally. It is usually a small piece of unprocessed wood pulp that has been incorporated into the paper during manufacture, and is often referred to as a "natural inclusion." Many of these specks are minute, visible only from the gum side of the stamp, and as such are inconsequential. However, occasionally a large, dark speck will appear on the face side of a stamp in an area where there is little or no printing to help conceal it. This type

11

of speck is the most damaging, and adversely affects a stamp's value. Paper specks cannot usually be removed without damaging the stamp.

Stains

Stains come in all sizes, colors, and shapes, and result from an infinite number of sources. Some can be completely removed, and some cannot. It is difficult, if not impossible, to know ahead of time with any degree of certainty which stains might be successfully removed. Hence, anyone considering the purchase of a stained stamp should always assume the stain to be permanent.

Stains can be removed by something as simple as a soft eraser, or they may require equipment as complex as that found in chemical laboratories. The removal may take only a few seconds, or it may take days. An attempt to remove a stain may yield a totally restored stamp, one that is free of any trace of the original stain, and one whose gum and original color is unaltered. Conversely, the attempt may also result in a ruined stamp.

The successful removal of stains from a stamp requires a thorough understanding of the nature of printing inks, solvents, paper stability, and of the stains themselves. The removal of specific stains has been documented in the literature.[5]

Repairs

There are two additional repairs which deserve special attention in this chapter.

[5]An article entitled "Postage Stamp Restoration," by Robert Fellows, appeared in two parts in the April 7, 1973; and April 14, 1973 issues of *Stamps* magazine. In this article, Mr. Fellows discusses the required equipment and solvents for the removal of a great number of stains including: pencil, grease, adhesive tape, wax, tar, tobacco, crayon, oil, ink (various types), mildew, etc.

Rebacking

Sometimes the only way to satisfactorily repair a stamp with numerous faults is to add an entirely new back to the stamp. This major repair requires time and skill, and therefore it is usually reserved for stamps of considerable value.

First the stamp is thoroughly cleaned. Then it is sanded or shaved down until it is as uniformly thin as possible. In this step of the process, all but the deepest thins are eliminated. This reduction of the stamp's overall thickness is also necessary so that the finished stamp will be approximately the correct thickness after the new back is added. General repairs such as closing tears, pressing out creases, or filling deep thins are also made. A new, oversize back is then glued to the stamp. If the stamp is unused, or if the cancel has been removed, it is usually regummed. Finally, the stamp is trimmed or carefully reperforated, using the original holes on the front as guides.

There are two ways to detect rebacked stamps. The first is to place the stamp face down in watermark fluid and carefully observe how quickly the paper absorbs the fluid. Sound stamps will do so very quickly, usually within a fraction of a second. A rebacked stamp, however, will often appear quite white, slowly darkening from the edges to the center as the paper fibers absorb the fluid. Rapid absorption is prevented by the adhesive used to attach the added back. To view this effect more clearly, there should be enough fluid in the tray so that the stamp does not rest on the bottom of the tray, and the stamp should be dropped flatly onto the surface of the fluid.

A rebacked stamp can at times be detected by examining the stamp's edge very carefully with a 15x or better magnifying glass. If the stamp is perforated, often the added back will be visible as a second layer where a new perforation hole is not exactly in the same position as an existing hole. Imperforate stamps do not afford the examiner this advantage, and at times it is difficult to detect the added back by this method.

Looking at a rebacked stamp edgewise under high magnification will sometimes reveal the second layer. In addition, examination under ultraviolet light will at times result in a marked difference in appearance of the front and back of such a stamp. However, if the stamp has also been regummed, this difference is often effectively hidden.

Added Margins

Adding a margin or margins to a stamp is a repair associated primarily with imperforate issues, although such an addition is not limited to them exclusively. This repair gives a stamp the appearance of having full margins. If part of the original stamp design is missing, it must be painted in after the new margin is added.

At times the additional margin is so skillfully applied that it is not visible simply by looking at the stamp. In watermark fluid the added margin will often appear lighter than the rest of the stamp, particularly at the joining line. If design parts have also been added, a high power magnifier and an ultraviolet light may help to detect them. Sometimes four new margins can be added to a stamp by trimming the stamp to the exact shape of its design and attaching it to a new back. This repair is described in more detail in the chapter on altered stamps.

Chapter Two

GUM

Introduction

There was a time when the term "original gum" (OG) was not used very often, for a stamp either had gum or it did not. Whether a stamp was hinged or unhinged was also of little consequence.

Today, one need only pick up any trade paper to see that times have changed. Often today's collector is more concerned with a stamp's gum than with any other feature. This concern is reflected in ever-increasing prices for those stamps described as being never-hinged (NH) with original gum. The increasing prices only generate more concern, and while certainly the merits of such a cycle are debatable, one fact emerges which must be carefully considered: in today's market, most OG/NH stamps command prices that are significantly higher than their hinged counterparts. It has therefore become quite profitable for the faker to regum stamps whose original gum has either become flawed in some way or lost entirely. In this chapter, two major questions will be considered:

> *Is the gum original to the stamp?*
>
> *If the gum is original, are there any gum flaws which may adversely affect the value of the stamp?*

Characteristics of Original Gum

United States stamps have always been printed on two general types of printing presses, the flat-bed press and the rotary press. Flat-bed presses were used for all issues until about 1914, when experiments were begun using a rotary type press. By about 1935, all stamps with only a few exceptions were printed on rotary presses, as they allowed for faster and more economical production. This chapter will not detail the two printing processes, but rather discuss the resulting differences in appearance of the gum on stamps produced by the two methods.[1]

Gum Characteristics of Stamps Produced on Flat-Bed Presses

Stamps printed on flat-bed presses are generally older than rotary press issues, and therefore they often have gum that varies in color, texture, and translucency from issue to issue and even within issues. These variations are the results of several factors. Prior to 1894, United States stamps were printed by private contractors, and many different gum formulas were used. In the attempt to improve such diverse qualities as viscosity, drying time, shrinkage, and humidity stability, each contractor developed its own gum recipe. It can also be assumed that the quality control on early gum mixtures was not as rigid as the control on later issues; therefore, differences can exist in gum of a given formula. Finally, in comparison with many rotary press issues, most flat plate stamps have been exposed to a longer period and greater range of atmospheric and storage conditions; thus the appearance of flat plate gum will often vary considerably.

The paper that was fed into the flat-bed press was dampened prior to printing, and while still damp, but before going into the dryers, gum was applied to the sheets. During the drying process the paper had a tendency to shrink, and the gum, while it too experienced shrinkage, did not necessarily do so at the same rate as

---

[1] Detailed accounts of flat and rotary printing processes can be found in *Fundamentals of Philately* by L.N. and M. Williams (State College, PA, 1971).

the paper. The results of this uneven shrinkage are variously called "gum creases," "gum bends," or "gum wrinkles," often preceded by the adjective "natural." Indeed, they are a natural result of the manufacturing process, and while in some instances they are of little or no consequence, they can in their extremes affect the value of a stamp considerably.

The most common feature of flat plate gum is a pattern of what appears to be slight creases running in straight lines at varying angles across an entire sheet of stamps. They may be parallel, but more often than not they intersect at various points (fig. 2.1). A typical sheet may have only two or three such creases, or it may have a dozen or more. It is important to realize that these creases

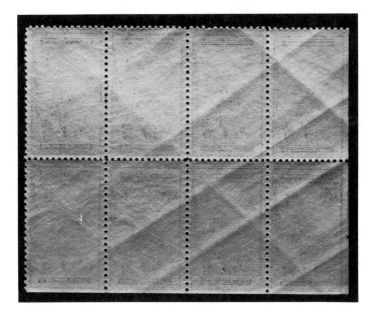

Figure 2.1. Gum Creases. Characteristic of stamps printed on flat-bed presses, gum creases are the result of the uneven shrinkage during drying of the paper and the gum. They are often only a surface phenomenon and as such will not be visible in watermark fluid.

are usually only a surface phenomenon, and upon immersion in watermark fluid, most will disappear completely. On some stamps, however, this natural occurrence can be severe enough to deform the paper fibers of the stamp (fig. 2.2). This type of gum crease is visible in watermark fluid as a dark line, and the darker the line the more severe the crease. In its extreme form, a gum crease can severely wrinkle the stamp paper so that the crease is visible from the face side of the stamp. To become more familiar with gum creases, one should examine the gum side of sheets printed on flat-bed presses. Gum creases can also occur on rotary press stamps, but they are uncommon.

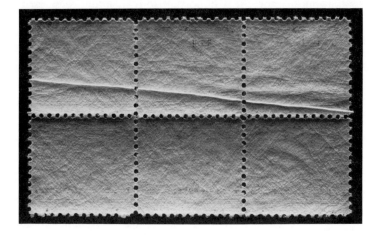

Figure 2.2. Gum Crease. The paper fibers of the stamp are deformed by this natural, though damaging occurrence. Such a crease will appear in watermark fluid as a dark line.

Another natural phenomenon associated with stamps printed on flat-bed presses is the gum skip. Gum skips are small areas where no gum has been deposited. They are usually irregular in shape and can vary in size from a pinhead to the size of a dime, and sometimes, though rarely, they are even larger. They occur most frequently near the edge of a sheet, thus they are often encountered on plate blocks (fig. 2.3).

18

Figure 2.3. Gum Skips. The lighter areas are portions of the stamps where no gum was deposited. They often occur near the edge of a sheet, thus they are commonly encountered on flat plate printed plate blocks.

Gum Characteristics of Stamps Produced on Rotary Presses

The quality and consistency of gum used on rotary press issues is generally far superior to that found on flat plate printed stamps. Differences in appearance of the original gum within a particular issue are usually minimal. When they do exist, they are generally due to atmospheric and storage effects.

However, there is one characteristic of rotary press gum that can result in a marked difference in the gum's appearance, even within the same issue. It is known as "ridged gum." Rotary press stamps are printed on a continuous roll of paper, and the metal roll which applies the gum to the paper has a finely threaded surface. The gum is applied in streams which usually, but not always, flow together to form a smooth, continuous surface before reaching the

19

dryers. If this coalescence does not take place the pattern of gum streams hardens, resulting in the phenomenon of ridged gum (fig. 2.4.)

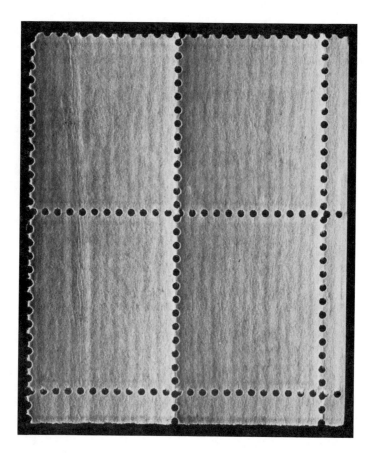

Figure 2.4. Ridged Gum. A feature of some rotary press stamps, ridged gum occurs when the gum, which is applied in streams by a finely threaded roller, fails to coalesce before reaching the dryers.

Another prominent feature of the gum on rotary press stamps is the presence of gum breakers. These are lightly impressed, parallel ridges occurring at regular intervals. They are applied by a special gum breaker roller from the face side of the stamp after printing and before perforating. Their purpose is to prevent the paper from curling after it is cut into post office panes. They should not be confused with gum ridges. The gum breakers are almost perpendicular to any gum ridges that may be present, and their spacing can vary from about 5.5 to 22 millimeters (fig. 2.5).

Gum Disturbances

The broad array of gum disturbances encountered on many stamps generally results from handling and storage conditions after the stamp has left the printer. This section will discuss some of those disturbances.

Hinging

Rarely was a stamp mounted in an album with anything but a hinge prior to the mid-1930's. Collections formed in the very early years of this century were usually mounted with heavy paper hinges or with hinges made from linen. Sometimes the stamp was simply glued to the album page. The total preservation of gum was not a prime concern of early collectors. Stamps of that period which exist today in never-hinged condition are most often obtained from blocks or sheets where only some of the stamps were hinged, or from accumulations that were never placed in an album. Because of their prohibitive cost, early high face value stamps were not frequently saved as multiples, and this accounts for their present scarcity in never-hinged condition.

The development of the peelable hinge allowed a stamp to be mounted and removed with only minimal disturbance to the gum. However today, most collectors would probably not hinge an expensive stamp, even one that had been previously hinged, and the

21

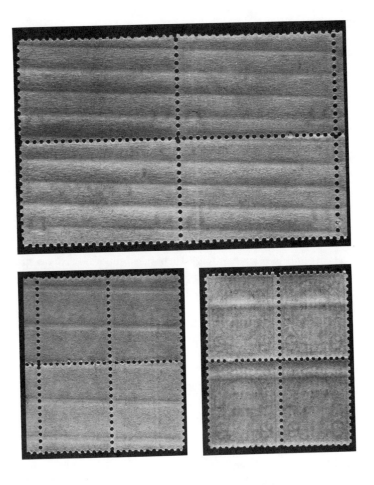

Figure 2.5. Gum Breakers. To keep rotary printed panes from curling, gum breakers were impressed from the face side using special gum breaker rollers. The three examples shown have the breakers spaced 5.5, 12, and 22 mm apart, respectively.

availability of many types of mounts makes this possible. Mounts also provide extra protection against damage, and some believe they provide a desirable aesthetic appearance as well.

22

Since the condition of the gum has reached a position of major importance in today's market, it is not surprising that dealers and collectors have developed terms that accurately describe the gum side of a stamp. Accordingly, stamps are not simply described as hinged or never-hinged, but many degrees of hinging are defined. Typical descriptions might be as follows:

> *Never-Hinged (NH).* There is absolutely no trace of any hinge mark. Care should be taken to examine the NH stamp in a good light at various angles, since attempts to remove extremely light hinge marks are sometimes made. Hinge marks do not always appear at the top center of a stamp. For example, stamps taken from blocks that were hinged in the center could have hinge marks in any corner.

> *Very Lightly Hinged (VLH).* Only the barest trace of a small hinge mark should be visible. Absolutely no hinge remnant should be present.

> *Lightly Hinged (LH).* No hinge remnant should be present; however, the hinge mark will be easily visible.

> *Hinged (H).* A significant portion of the stamp will show hinge marks, and there may be some tiny pieces of the hinge still adhering to the stamp.

> *Heavily Hinged (HH).* Remnants of one or more hinges may be present. If no remnants are present, the gum will be quite disturbed from the removal of previous hinges.

The above descriptions are only examples of what might be found in the marketplace, and they will vary considerably among dealers and collectors. It is certainly possible, and in fact most likely, that what one person may consider lightly hinged, another may consider hinged. Each individual must develop a visual standard of what is acceptable and what is not.

The Proper Removal of a Hinge

The proper removal of an unsightly hinge can vastly improve the appearance of a stamp, and perhaps even aid in its preservation, since the paper fibers of a stamp are sometimes severely deformed by the presence of a hinge.

There is only one correct method to remove a hinge that has firmly adhered to the back of a stamp. With a good artist's watercolor brush, carefully paint the back of the adhered hinge with warm water. Be sure to paint the entire hinge without going over the edges. After about one minute, repeat the procedure. When the entire hinge shows signs of wrinkling, carefully blot the remaining water from the hinge. With the brush, lift a corner of the hinge, and then gently pull the hinge using a pair of tongs. If it does not lift off easily, repaint with more water, wait a bit, and then blot again before trying to remove the hinge. Some very old and thick paper hinges may take quite a few applications of water before they can be successfully removed. If, after the hinge has been removed, the gum is in small puddles, spread it about as evenly as possible with a slightly dampened brush, and allow the stamp to dry thoroughly. It will curl up while drying. However, it can be easily straightened out after it is completely dry by placing the stamp in a glassine envelope and pulling it gently over a relatively sharp edge, like that of a table. The final pull over the edge should be one that gives the stamp a slight natural curl to the gum side.

There are some potential dangers that exist anytime a hinge removal is attempted. If too little water is applied to the hinge, there is a danger of thinning the stamp when attempting to pull the hinge off. If too much water is used, the stamp fibers become saturated and the gum can pass through to the face side. The resulting "gum soak" is often similar in appearance to a grease stain, and if the stamp is held to a light, a gum soak can also resemble a thin. Unlike a thin, however, a gum soak will not be visible in watermark fluid. Gum soaks are most likely to occur at the perforations where the paper fibers are already broken, and extreme care should be taken in this area.

The proper removal of a hinge requires practice, patience, and a steady hand. Initial attempts, therefore, should be made on stamps of little value.

Miscellaneous Gum Faults

In addition to gum creases and gum soaks which have already been discussed, there are other gum faults which occur with some regularity. Page remnants are pieces of an album page which have adhered to the back of a stamp. Large remnants can usually be removed by following the same procedure as that for the removal of a hinge, but it is very difficult to remove numerous tiny remnants that have adhered to a stamp. Page remnants are particularly unsightly when they are a dark color (fig. 2.6). Stamps with page remnants often have tiny thins as well, and such stamps should be examined carefully.

The term "disturbed gum" is a general one, often used in describing a stamp whose gum faults have resulted from undetermined causes. The more severe the disturbance, the more difficult it

Figure 2.6. Page Remnants. Portions of the album page still adhering to a stamp are commonly referred to as page remnants. In this example the page was a dark color so the remnant is particularly noticeable.

can be to evaluate whether the gum is original. Occasionally a poorly regummed stamp may be offered as one with disturbed original gum.

Heat can affect the color and quality of gum. Prolonged exposure to warm temperatures can result in what is often called "toned" gum; that is, gum that has yellowed or browned. Cracking may or may not be present. Collectors will sometimes remove the gum from an early issue rather than risk the stamp being destroyed by chemical or cracking action.

Regummed Stamps

Stamps are usually regummed for the following reasons:

*To add gum to a stamp that has lost its
original gum.*

*To make a hinged stamp appear to be a
never-hinged stamp.*

*To conceal defects and/or repairs in a
stamp.*

Depending upon the proficiency of the regummer, the detection
of regummed stamps can either be quite easy or very difficult. The
skilled faker is aware of the telltale signs of a regummed stamp and
will try to eliminate them.

Two important points should be kept in mind when examining
a stamp for regumming. First, and perhaps most significant, is the
fact that all United States stamps were gummed before being perforated. The regummer, however, has no choice but to apply gum
to a stamp after it has been perforated.[2] Second, the gum formula
used by the regummer is rarely the same as that used by the printer.
Thus, there are important differences between stamps with original
gum and those that have been regummed.

In attempting to determine whether a stamp is regummed, examine the gum carefully, comparing it with other stamps from the
same issue. While one may not have the opportunity to examine
many five-dollar Columbian stamps, there are numerous one-cent
and two-cent values of the same series available. Gum can vary considerably from issue to issue, so one should not compare the gum
on a Columbian stamp with the gum on a Pan-American stamp.
One must also remember that gum variations can and do exist, even
among stamps of the same issue. However, after examining many
stamps of a given issue, these variations should fall within certain
limits. There is no substitute for experience in judging the originali-
ty of a stamp's gum.

The stamp should also be examined **face up** under a good light,

---

[2]The only exceptions would be those imperforate issues that had lost their
original gum and were regummed prior to being reperforated.

using a 15x magnifier or a widefield microscope. Carefully search the perforation tips for any gum that may have adhered to the broken paper fibers. The semicircular portions of the perforations should also be examined carefully for any gum that may have spilled over from the back during the regumming process. If any of these signs are present, there is an excellent chance that the stamp has been regummed. It should be noted that one may detect some or all of these signs directly opposite a hinge mark, particularly if the hinge is close to the perforations. The softening of the gum and subsequent pressure on the stamp while it is being hinged and mounted often forces a bit of the original gum to the face side of the stamp. Some examiners will lightly rub the perforation tips with their fingers to determine if the tips have the soft feel of a genuinely gummed and separated stamp. A regummed stamp will often feel quite sharp. This procedure should only be undertaken with the greatest of care, since a perforation tip can easily be damaged or broken.

The fact that the tips are free from all gum and have the correct feel is not reason enough to claim that the stamp has original gum. If the item was originally from a large multiple and had been separated after regumming, the perforation tips would have the proper appearance. In addition, regummers realize that perforation tips which show excess gum adhering to the paper fibers are perhaps the surest clue in determining whether a stamp has been regummed, and they have developed methods to remove this telltale sign. Therefore, examination of both the perforation tips and the semicircular holes is absolutely necessary.

The use of an ultraviolet light can be helpful in determining whether a stamp is regummed. Since the regummer does not normally have access to gum of the exact composition as that of the original formula, he will use gum that looks as much as possible like the original when viewed under normal light.[3] Its appearance

[3] It is sometimes possible to regum a stamp with gum of the original formula. The regumming solution is made by soaking pieces of originally gummed selvedge in water and then evaporating this solution to a workable consistency. Only very small amounts of gum are available by this method, and therefore, it is generally reserved for stamps of considerable value.

under ultraviolet light, however, is sometimes quite different. Here again, the stamp in question must be compared with copies that are known to have original gum.

Often during the examination of the gum side of a flat plate printed stamp, tiny specks the same color as the stamp itself will be noticed. They may appear to be in a seemingly random pattern, or look as though they follow the design of the stamp itself, only reversed. These specks of color are the result of sheets of stamps being piled one upon the other after they were printed, before the ink was fully dry. These specks are therefore under the gum, and while they are not directly related to the gum, they are nonetheless observed during the examination of the gum side of a flat press stamp (fig. 2.7). The commonly held belief that any stamp showing these color specks must have original gum is clearly false.

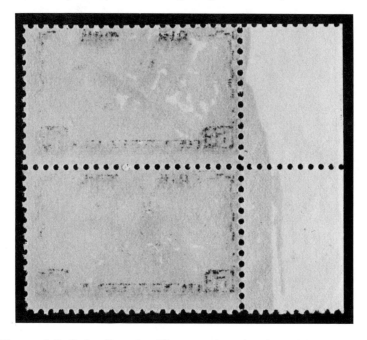

Figure 2.7. Color Specks. The specks of color which in this example appear to follow the design of the stamp, only reversed, are under the gum and as such are not an indication that the stamp has original gum.

Chapter Three

PERFORATION

Introduction

Since 1857, United States stamps have been perforated to facilitate their separation. This chapter will not go into detail regarding perforating methods and machines, as detailed accounts are available elsewhere.[1] It is necessary, however, during the examination of a stamp, to be familiar with some of the basic principles of perforation. The detection of fraudulently perforated stamps often depends on knowing what legitimately perforated stamps look like, and why they appear as they do.

Perforating Machines

There are two general methods of perforating stamps, stroke and rotary. Stroke perforators include a pattern of pins arranged on a flat head and a matching counterplate drilled with corresponding holes. The perforating process consists of placing a sheet or sheets of paper between the head and the counterplate and then simply lowering the head vertically downward until the pins have passed through the paper into the counterplate (fig. 3.1). This

---

[1]Williams, pp. 501-629.

downward vertical motion of the head is called a stroke, giving us the general name for this type of perforator. The stroke perforator, however, was never used to perforate United States stamps.

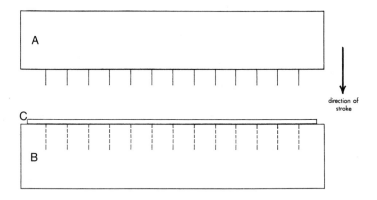

Figure 3.1 Stroke Perforation. Perforation is accomplished when the perforating pins on the head (A) descend vertically through the paper (C) and into the matching holes of the counterplate (B).

Rotary perforators were used by both the Bureau of Engraving and Printing as well as by the private banknote companies that printed United States stamps prior to 1894. The two basic parts of the rotary perforator are the perforating wheel and the counterpart wheel. The perforating wheel consists of equally spaced, tiny pins and the counterpart wheel of matching holes (fig. 3.2). There are two basic types of rotary perforators, one-way and two-way. In a one-way rotary perforator, the paper is fed into the wheels first in one direction and then in the other to effect the complete perforation of the sheet (fig. 3.3). With the development of the rotary printing press, not to be confused with the rotary perforator, refinements in perforating equipment were needed so that the continuous web of paper could be perforated in both the longitudinal and lateral directions while the web necessarily traveled in a single direction. The two-way perforator developed for use on such a rotary press first perforates longitudinally using standard perforating wheels. Slightly further down the web it adds lateral perforations through the use of a row of pins arranged on a rotating cylinder. The pins mate with a corresponding cylinder drilled with lateral rows of matching holes (fig. 3.4). The overall perforating method, therefore, is still rotary. In a rotary perforator the actual cutting of the holes occurs, not with a downward vertical motion as with the stroke perforator, but with a somewhat angular motion that produces considerable shear in the paper as it is cut. This seemingly technical difference in the production of the holes will be of primary importance in the detection of reperforated stamps.

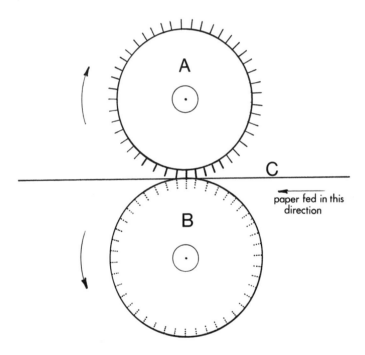

Figure 3.2. Rotary Perforation. The perforating wheel (A) consists of equally spaced pins, and the counterpart wheel (B) of matching holes. The paper (C) is perforated by being fed into the rotating wheels.

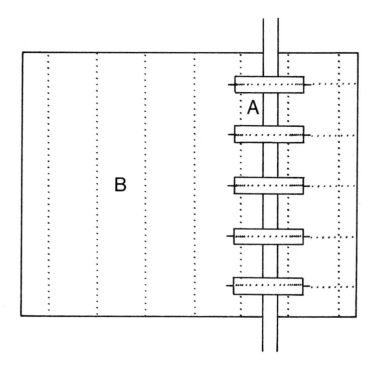

Figure 3.3. One-Way Rotary Perforator. The sheet of stamps is perforated one direction at a time. After a first pass through the perforating wheels (A), the sheet (B) is rotated ninety degrees and passed through again to effect the complete perforation of the sheet.

Detection of Reperforated Stamps

The term "reperforated" as used in this book refers to the addition of perforations by private parties after the stamp has left the printer.[2] While it would be more accurate to describe such stamps

---

[2] The only exceptions will be those stamps which were privately perforated by

as fraudulently perforated, the term reperforated is widely used to mean the same thing.

Reperforating is usually done for the purpose of making a stamp appear more valuable than it actually is, and the major reasons for reperforating are summarized below:

> *To make a given stamp appear to be a totally different stamp. Such a stamp is often called a "manufactured" stamp.*
>
> *To remove the unperforated or straight edge that often exists on sheets of stamps printed on flat-bed presses.*
>
> *To alter the original centering of a stamp.*
>
> *To improve the appearance of a stamp that has a missing or short perforation.*

At the outset it should be noted that the detection of reperforated stamps can be a difficult task. Faced with a skillful reperforating job, even an expert will sometimes have difficulty making an accurate judgment. There exist, however, a great number of reperforated stamps in the market today that the collector can learn to detect.

Required Equipment

Perforation gauges are used to determine the number of perforations within a distance of two centimeters. Most gauges are graduated by halves or fourths, but one, the "Instanta" manufactured by Stanley Gibbons of Great Britain, allows the user to deter-

---

various companies early in the twentieth century for use in their private stamp vending machines. Commonly referred to as private vending machine coils, they are not among this chapter's subjects.

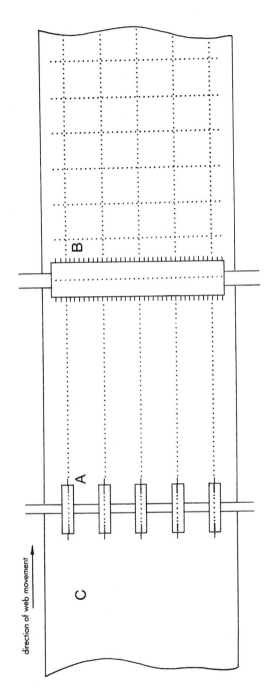

direction of web movement

Figure 3.4. Two-Way Rotary Perforator. The continuously moving web of paper (C) is first perforated longitudinally using standard perforating wheels (A). Further down the web the lateral perforations are added by a rotating bar perforator (B).

mine precisely the exact gauge. A catalog listing of ten perforations per two centimeters, for example, is usually only an approximation, the actual number being somewhat greater or less. The "Perf-Vu" gauge copyrighted by Voncorp of Florida and designed for use only with United States stamps shows three different gauges for stamps generally categorized as being perforated eleven, namely those with perforation hole center-to-center dimensions of 0.070, 0.072, and 0.073 inches. An accompanying brochure describes the particular issues associated with each gauge.

The use of a perforation gauge to detect reperforated stamps is limited by the fact that most fakes approximate the correct gauge. Unless the exact gauge of the genuine stamp is known, only the crudest of reperforated stamps can be detected. One of the best "gauges," therefore, is a genuinely perforated copy of the same stamp or a stamp from the same series as the one in question. By placing the genuine copy on top of or next to the questionable stamp, very precise measurements of gauge and hole size can be made. Correct hole size is important, for sometimes the reperforated stamp will gauge correctly, but err in the size of the hole (fig. 3.5).

In addition to a perforation gauge, a magnifier of high quality is necessary. A wide field microscope of 30x is excellent, but a glass of 15x is sufficient.

Finally, a grid of straight lines ruled into a piece of clear plastic is helpful, as is the " 'Thirkell' Philatelic Position Finder" manufactured by Stanley Gibbons.

General Considerations

The detection of reperforated stamps is easier when the item in question is a multiple such as a block, a coil pair, or a strip. The multiple affords the opportunity to examine the complete perforation hole, and the first step in attempting to determine if the stamp is reperforated is the careful examination of the holes themselves.

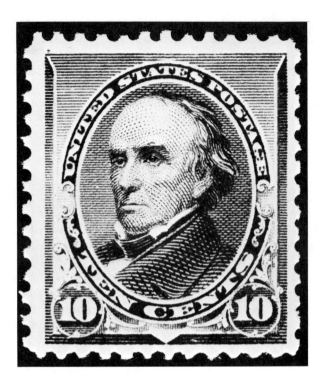

Figure 3.5. Reperforated at the Right. Even though the gauge is correct, the perforation holes on the right side are too small when compared with those of the other three sides.

As indicated earlier in this chapter, stroke and rotary perforating machines make significantly different types of holes. The key fact to remember is that while United States stamps have always been perforated with a rotary perforator of some type, most reperforated stamps are made with a technique that is similar to the operation of a stroke perforator. The action of the rotary perforator first involves cutting at an angle, then almost pulling the paper along, and finally, shearing the hole from the paper itself. The result is a hole that is not quite round, but often slightly oval, and one in which the inner edge of a particular side shows ragged paper fibers as a result of the shearing action (fig. 3.6). By contrast, the hole resulting from a stroke perforator is very round and very clean, since it is produced by a sharp, vertical downward cutting action. If upon examination under a magnifier, the perforation holes of a United States stamp appear perfectly round and clean, it is likely that the stamp has been reperforated (fig. 3.7).

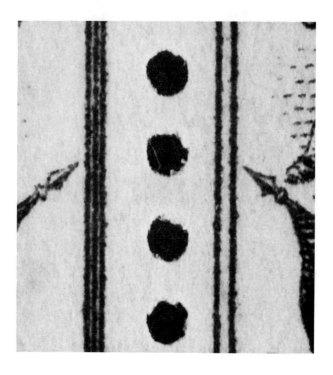

Figure 3.6. A Typical Rotary Perforated Hole. The hole is not quite round and part of the inner edge shows ragged paper fibers, a result of the shearing action produced during this method of perforation.

During the rotary perforating process, the paper between the perforation holes is creased very slightly. This natural occurrence can be detected in a multiple by lightly sliding it between the thumb

Figure 3.7. A Bogus Perforation Hole. The hole appears too round and clean and bears little resemblance to a genuine rotary perforated hole.

and middle finger, perpendicular to the perforations between the two stamps. On the gum side there should be a slight bump at the perforations, and although at times it is quite faint, this bump is indicative of a genuinely perforated stamp. Most reperforated stamps will be completely smooth. This procedure is particularly useful with coil pairs.

Single stamps are always more difficult to analyze because there are no complete perforation holes to examine, but only "half holes." A valid generalization for reperforated stamps is that, as a rule, they are usually reperforated only on one side, sometimes two, but very seldom on three or four sides.[3] Thus, there exists the advantage of having two or three genuinely perforated sides with which to make comparisons. On genuinely perforated stamps the perforation holes should be the same size on all four sides.[4] The holes should be of similar sharpness; one or two sides should not stand out because of extremely clean and clear perforations, while the other sides appear more ragged (fig. 3.8). The raggedness within each hole should be properly positioned and fairly consistent within the row. The perforations on older stamps will often appear to have a certain softness that results from age and handling.

Figure 3.8. Reperforated at the Top. The sharp and clean appearance of the perforation holes at the top are an indication that this stamp has been reperforated. Compare the perforations carefully with those of the remaining three sides.

[3]This does not include those commonly manufactured stamps such as Scott Nos. 461 or 519, which are reperforated on all four sides.

[4]It is possible to find a genuinely perforated stamp with an occasional perforation hole that differs in size from the others. This is the result of a broken perforating pin having been replaced with a new pin of incorrect size.

Genuine perforation holes should be in a straight line.[5] Some stamps are reperforated one hole at a time, and as a result the holes are generally out of line. Usually on this crude type of reperforation the gauge is also questionable.

Perforation tips should not be ragged on some sides and sharp on others. This is often the case when the reperforator, lacking enough space in the margin to add a row of full holes to the stamp, is forced to put in a row of half holes, making the stamp appear as if it were separated with a pair of scissors (fig. 3.9). However, skillful reperforators have learned how to rough up these sharp per-

Figure 3.9. Reperforated at the Left. The extremely sharp appearance of the perforation tips indicate that this stamp was probably a straight-edge copy before it was reperforated. Note also the sharp and clean nature of the holes themselves, another indication that the stamp has been reperforated.

[5]A genuinely perforated stamp may have an occasional perforation hole out of line. This irregularity is caused by a bent perforating pin.

foration tips, making them appear as if they had been separated from an adjoining stamp in the usual manner.

Reperforated Flat-Bed Press Stamps

Of all United States issues, those printed on flat-bed presses are the most frequently reperforated. The reasons are clear. Such issues constitute the vast majority of valuable stamps; they exist with natural straight edges, whereas rotary issues do not; and most importantly, fully imperforate issues exist which can be reperforated to resemble other more valuable issues.

Flat plate printed coils as well as two fully perforated issues have been the traditional targets of the reperforators. The availability of less expensive imperforate issues has resulted in the market being flooded with manufactured stamps. Fake coils can also be made by trimming fully perforated stamps from sheets or booklet panes. Table 3.1 lists those flat plate printed issues which are commonly manufactured.

There are some important, overall characteristics of genuine perforations found on flat plate printed stamps that can be logically deduced from a knowledge of the perforating machines used for their production. United States stamps printed on flat-bed presses were perforated in-line by one-way rotary perforators. That is to say, the sheets were perforated one direction at a time. From this fact, several important perforation features can be explained. The slightly oval holes produced by the one-way rotary perforator are "stretched" in the direction of the row they are in. The position of the ragged edges within each hole will also be fairly consistent within each row. For example, perforation holes at the left and right of a stamp will exhibit this raggedness at the top or bottom of the hole, and the perforations at the top and bottom of a stamp will be ragged at the left or right (fig. 3.10). Knowledge of these characteristics can be useful when trying to determine whether an individual stamp has been reperforated on a particular side.

Another point to consider in the examination of the perfora-

Table 3.1

Commonly "Manufactured" Flat Plate Issues of the United States

This stamp can be "manufactured"	by reperforating this stamp,	by trimming the top and bottom or sides of this stamp,	by trimming stamps from this booklet pane*
Scott No.	Scott No.	Scott No.	Scott No.
316	314	300	300b
317	315	304	--
318	314	300	**
321	320	319	319g
322	[320a (die II) 320b (die II)	319f (die II)	**
348	343	331	331a
349	344	332	332a
350	346	334	--
351	347	335	--
352	343	331	**
353	344	332	**
354	346	334	--
355	347	335	--
356	--	338	--
385	383	374	374a
386	384	375	375a
387	383	374	**
388	384	375	**
389	--	376	--
390	383	--	--
391	384	--	--
392	383	--	--
393	384	--	--
410	408	--	--
411	409	--	--

Table 3.1 (continued)

This stamp can be "manufactured"	by reperforating this stamp,	by trimming the top and bottom or sides of this stamp	by trimming stamps from this booklet pane*
Scott No.	Scott No.	Scott No.	Scott No.
412	408	--	--
413	409	--	--
441	408	424	424d
442	409	425	425e
443	408	424	**
444	409	425	**
445	--	426	--
446	--	427	--
447	--	428	--
461	409	--	--
519	344	--	--

* Fake coils manufactured from booklet panes are readily detectable by checking the watermark. Genuine coils are watermarked horizontally, while those made from booklet panes will have a vertical watermark.

**While it is possible to find horizontal coils manufactured from booklet panes, they are rarely encountered, since in addition to trimming the top and bottom, the sides would also have to be reperforated.

tions on flat plate printed stamps is the relative position of adjoining perforation rows. In figure 3.11, note that the top perforation hole in each row of the bogus pair is exactly the same distance from the pair's top edge. However, since each of the perforating wheels is a separate entity, the only common part being the shaft to which they are attached, such a coincidence would be highly unlikely. Manufactured coils often have perforations of this type, probably because the faker sets up the reperforating operation using some

Figure 3.10. Genuine In-Line Rotary Perforated Holes.
Characteristics of the overall configuration are important in making a judgment regarding the authenticity of a stamp's perforation holes. Note here that the holes appear slightly "stretched" in the direction of perforation, and that the edge raggedness is fairly consistent within the rows.

type of jig. Compare the perforations on the fake coil with those of the genuine pair shown in figure 3.12.

Finally, a stamp perforated on a one-way perforator need not have its vertical and horizontal perforations exactly perpendicular. The chance of a sheet being fed into the perforating machine at an angle other than exactly ninety degrees to the previously perforated rows is certainly possible. Thus, a stamp cannot be dismissed as fake simply because it is less than square. The perforation rows, however, should be essentially parallel to each other, and single stamps or multiples where this is not true should be regarded with suspicion (fig. 3.13).

46

Figure 3.11. Fake Coil Pair. In this manufactured coil pair of Scott No. 443, made from #408, note that the top hole in each row is exactly the same distance from the pair's top edge. This occurrence would be most unlikely in a genuine coil pair.

Figure 3.12. Genuine Coil Pair. The position of the top hole in each row relative to the pair's top edge varies in this genuine coil pair of Scott No. 445. Such random placement is expected in genuine coils.

Figure 3.13. Reperforated at the Left. In addition to having a sharper appearance, the perforations at the left are not quite parallel to those of the middle row or those at the right.

Reperforating a single stamp to remove the natural straight edge found on many flat plate printed issues has become a common practice. However, due to different plate configurations, not all issues exist with straight edges possible on all four sides. Table 3.2 indicates which sides of a particular issue can have a straight edge, and therefore deserve special attention. While it is possible to find a Trans-Mississippi stamp that has been reperforated on the top or bottom, perhaps with the aim of improving the centering, the majority of fraudulent perforations will be found on the left or right sides, where the natural straight edges occur.

Although the best way to detect reperforated stamps is to examine carefully the holes themselves, there are those flat plate printed stamps which must often pass other tests as well. Knowledge of the criteria described below can be of great help in correctly judging some stamps' authenticity.

Color. Some issues are known to exist in certain predominant colors, and very often a manufactured stamp is immediately suspect simply because of its color. The following information may prove helpful, but be aware that there are exceptions.

Stamp (Scott No.)	Predominant Genuine Colors	Bogus Colors
385,387,392	Green, Dark Green	Yellow-Green
411, 413,	Carmine, Dark	Carmine Rose,
442, 444,	Carmine, Red (444)	Rose-Red, Dark Rose-Red, Scarlet
461	Pale Carmine, Carmine	same as above

Spacing. In an attempt to solve perforating problems created by uneven paper shrinkage, the Bureau of Engraving and Printing carried out experiments using plates with various spacings between the stamps. Details of these experiments are available in the literature.[6] Let it suffice to say that two coil issues, Scott Nos. 392 and 393, were made only from plates having a uniform spacing between the stamps of 2.75 mm. Coils of these issues that measure approximately 2.0 mm between are generally considered to be bogus, having been manufactured by reperforating printings of Scott Nos. 383 and 384, respectively.

Coil Edges. Fake coils, made by trimming genuine sheet stamps, while not technically a reperforating problem, deserve discussion in this section. At times, such fakes are difficult to detect, since the perforation holes are genuine in all respects. Therefore, the unperforated edge of the coil should be examined closely. To say that genuine coils have a look and feel to the edge which is difficult to fake is true, but probably not very helpful. The edges of a genuine coil have a softness and shape to them which have resulted from age and handling and from their being cut with a cir-

[6]Max G. Johl. *United States Postage Stamps 1902-1935* (Lawrence, MA, 1976).

Table 3.2

Positions of Natural Straight Edges for Selected United States Issues

Issue	Scott No.	Straight Edge Position
1890-93 Issue		
1c, 2c	219, 219D, 220	All Four Sides
3c - 90c	221 - 229	Left or Right
Columbian Issue		
1c, 2c	230, 231	All Four Sides
3c - $5	232 - 245	Top or Bottom
1894 Issue		
1c - 5c, 10c	246 - 255, 258	All Four Sides
6c, 8c, 15c - $5	256, 257, 259 - 263	Left or Right
1895 Issue		
1c, 2c, 3c*, 10c	264 - 268, 273	All Four Sides
4c - 8c, 15c - $5	269 - 272, 274 - 278	Left or Right
1898 Issue		
1c, 2c, 4c*, 10c*	279 - 280, 282C, 283	All Four Sides
5c, 6c, 15c	281, 282, 284	Left or Right
Trans-Mississippi Issue		
1c - $2	285 - 293	Left or Right
Pan-American Issue		
1c - 10c	294 - 299	Top or Bottom
1902-03 Issue		
1c - 13c, 15c*	300 - 309	All Four Sides
50c - $5	310 - 313	Left or Right
Louisiana Purchase Issue		
1c - 10c	323 - 327	Left or Right
Jamestown Issue		
1c - 5c	328 - 330	Top or Bottom

Table 3.2 (continued)

Issue	Scott No.	Straight Edge Position
Franklin/Washington Definitive Issues, 1908-18		
1c - 30c	All	All Four Sides
50c Values	341, 422	Left or Right
	421, 440, 477, 517	All Four Sides
$1 Values	All	Left or Right
$2 Values	479	Left or Right
	523, 547	None
$5 Values	480	Left or Right
	524	None
1909 Commemoratives	367, 369, 370, 372	All Four Sides
Panama-Pacific Issue		
1c - 10c	397 - 404	All Four Sides
1922-25 Issue		
½c - 50c	550 - 570	All Four Sides
$1, $2	571, 572	Top or Bottom
$5	573	None
1918 Air Post Issue		
6c - 24c	C1 - C3	All Four Sides
1923 Air Post Issue		
8c - 24c	C4 - C6	All Four Sides
Graf Zeppelin Issue		
65c - $2.60	C13 - C15	None
Century of Progress Air Post		
50c	C18	None

*These stamps were printed from both 200 and 400-subject plates. Stamps from the 200-subject plates have watermarks that read vertically and natural straight edges can exist at the left or right. Stamps from the 400-subject plates have watermarks that read horizontally and straight edges can exist on all four sides.

cular rotating blade. Fakes cut with a razor blade simply do not feel or look the same. The imperforate edges of genuine coils need not be exactly parallel, as the cutting wheels were capable of some wobbling, and at times the paper had a tendency to gather up slightly during the cutting procedure. While this condition is never severe nor is it particularly common, it does exist, and one cannot dismiss a coil as fake because the edges are not exactly parallel. Marked irregularities along an edge, however, are not indicative of genuine coils, and they should be regarded with suspicion (fig. 3.14).

Figure 3.14. Fake Coil Pair. This manufactured pair of Scott No. 354 was made by trimming the top and bottom perforations from a pair of #334. The irregular trimming at the top and bottom is not indicative of genuine coils.

Coil Size. The size of the flat plate printed coil itself is an important feature to consider. Vertical coils generally measure at least 21.5 mm side to side, whereas horizontal coils are usually 25.0 mm top to bottom. These measurements are helpful only in detecting fake coils made from trimmed sheet stamps (fig. 3.15), as those fakes made from imperforates will generally measure correctly. These measurements are not absolutes, and doubtless there are genuine coils that do not meet these requirements.

Figure 3.15. Fake Coils. These are manufactured copies of Scott Nos. 318, 444, and 355, all made by trimming the top and bottom perforations from copies of #300, #425, and #335, respectively. Each is probably too short to be genuine, the #318 fake measuring 24.25 mm and the #355 and #444 fakes each measuring only 23.75 mm.

However, any coil that varies by more than 1.0 mm should be immediately suspect.

Centering. Genuine flat plate coils are not, as a rule, well centered. Fakes, as a rule, are beautifully centered. This simple fact should be kept in mind when examining these stamps. Superb genuine copies exist, but they are rare.

Reperforated Rotary Press Stamps

The numerous perforation problems encountered with flat plate issues fortunately do not exist with rotary press issues. There is only one imperforate rotary coil issue, Scott No. 459, and it is of considerable value. Reperforating it to resemble the less expensive coil, #453, would not be practical. Reperforating it to resemble the extremely rare vertical coil, #449, would not fool a knowledgeable collector, since the design sizes are considerably different. Number 459 is 19.5 to 20.0 mm wide, whereas #449 is only 18.5 to 19.0 mm wide. Number 449 is also slightly taller.

The most deceptive rotary press fakes are manufactured copies of the 1923 coil waste issues (Scott Nos. 578, 579) made by reperforating the issued coils (Scott Nos. 597, 599) at the top and bottom, with an eleven gauge perforation (fig. 3.16). A careful comparison of the perforations should be made using any copy of the perforated eleven flat plate series as a gauge, and the match must be exact with regard to gauge and hole size. The holes themselves should also be closely examined to see if they are typical of rotary line-perforated holes. Additionally, the perforation tips should not be sharp, but appear as if separated from an adjoining stamp. This last feature will often be faked by the experienced reperforator. Vertical pairs which gauge and measure correctly are always genuine, but the same cannot be said for horizontal pairs, since the fakes are made from horizontal coils. The one-cent value exists only in green and dark green, and yellow-green copies are most likely bogus.

Though easy to detect, another fairly prevalent fake is a

Figure 3.16. Fake Coil Waste Issues. These are copies of Scott Nos. 578 and 579, manufactured by reperforating the issued coils, #597 and #599, at the top and bottom.

manufactured copy of the two-cent perforated eleven coil waste issues of 1924 (Scott No. 595), made from the 1927 two-cent booklet pane (Scott No. 634d). Booklet panes often allow the faker the room to add additional rows of perforations at the left and right. By reperforating the pane with eleven gauge perforations at the sides, two bogus copies of #595 can be made. By also reperforating the bottom of a lower pane copy, a third fake can be made. The reason for the success of this fake is that most collectors do not believe there is any stamp from which a bogus #595 can be made, and technically there is not, for this fake errs slightly in the height of the stamp design, it being about one-half millimeter taller than the genuine stamp. Use a copy of the horizontal coil, #599, to make this comparison, as a genuine #595 will be exactly the same size as the coil (fig. 3.17). Fake mint copies of #595 made from booklet panes will also show one or two gum breakers on the back. These are not present on genuine copies of #595.

Following a procedure similar to that described for the two-

Figure 3.17. Fake Coil Waste. Shown left to right are copies of a booklet pane single, #634d, with ample margins for reperforating; a fake copy of Scott No. 595, made from such a booklet pane; a genuine copy of #595; a copy of the horizontal coil, #599, which measures the same size as #595.

cent coil waste issue (Scott No. 595), fakes of the much rarer one-cent coil waste issues (Scott Nos. 594, 596) are made from the one-cent booklet pane (Scott No. 632A). Again, a careful comparison using the issued coils (Scott Nos. 597 and 604, respectively) will show the design size of these fakes to be incorrect (fig. 3.18). Genuine one-cent coil waste issues exist only in dark green, and often the color of the manufactured copies is yellow-green.

A manufactured copy of the three-cent coil waste issue of 1919 (Scott No. 541) made by reperforating the top and bottom of the 1918 three-cent horizontal coil (Scott No. 494) is a fake which can be difficult to detect. Although the catalog values of the two issues are close, the faker profits by being able to manufacture a truly choice copy of the coil waste variety. This issue is known for its poor centering, and well-centered copies command substantial premiums. Therefore, beware of the perfectly centered copy. Check the top and bottom perforations in the same manner as described for fakes of #578 and #579.

The final group of reperforated stamps included in this section are manufactured copies of some of the perforated ten series of 1923-26 (Scott Nos. 581-91) made from corresponding values of the 1923-25 horizontal coils (Scott Nos. 597-603). These relatively new

Figure 3.18. Fake Coil Waste. This fake was made to resemble the rare one-cent coil waste variety, Scott No. 596, and was probably made from stamps in the one-cent booklet pane, #632a. The design size of the fake is incorrect, and this can easily be determined by comparing the fake with a copy of the one-cent vertical coil, #604, from which the genuine coil waste variety was made.

Figure 3.19. Fake Perforated Ten Issue. A copy of the horizontal coil, Scott No. 603 (at right), is reperforated at the top and bottom (center stamp) to resemble the scarcer perforated ten issue #591 (at left). This fake is easily detected, as it measures about three-quarters of a millimeter wider than the genuine stamp.

fakes are a direct result of the recent price increase of the perforated ten series, particularly the ten-cent value, #591. Although fakes of the other values are presently uncommon, collectors would be wise to keep their possibility in mind if the perforated ten values continue to rise sharply in price. Manufactured copies are easy to detect, as the design size is about three-quarters of a millimeter wider than on genuine copies. Unlike genuine copies, the fakes have no gum breakers, which on this issue are quite obvious and spaced about 5.5 mm apart (fig. 3.19).

Chapter Four

ALTERED STAMPS

Introduction

An altered stamp appears to be something it is not. Thus, reperforated, regummed, or repaired stamps qualify as altered stamps, and they have been the subjects of earlier chapters. This chapter will investigate other alterations which are either commonly encountered, or which pose significant problems in their detection. Some of these alterations will be applicable to any stamp, while others will be limited to a particular stamp or issue.

Alteration of Stamp Designs

Minute differences in a stamp's design can account for entirely separate catalog listings and values. When there are significant differences in the catalog values of similar stamps, a faker will sometimes try to manufacture the more valuable stamp by altering the design of the cheaper variety. Tiny design elements can be painted in with a fine artist's brush, and at times this alteration can be done so skillfully as to be unnoticeable to the naked eye. Design elements can also be removed by scraping off unwanted lines of color with a sharp instrument. Again, detection can be virtually impossible without the aid of a magnifying glass.

Design alterations can sometimes be detected by examining the stamp under ultraviolet light. Inks which appear to be identical in color under normal light, may at times look quite different when viewed under ultraviolet light. A good magnifier can be helpful in detecting areas where there may be evidence of scraping. Further confirmation of such scraping can sometimes be had by watching the area in question slowly air dry after the stamp has been removed from watermark fluid. The scraped paper fibers will often white-up quicker than the surrounding fibers.

The surest way to detect a design alteration, however, is to know what the genuine stamp design looks like. Whether due to a lack of knowledge on the part of the faker, or because of the complexity of the design, there are almost always parts of a stamp's original design that are not properly altered.

19th Century Issues

Perhaps the most commonly altered United States nineteenth century stamp designs are from the 1851-1861 issue. Many of the values exist as a number of distinct design types, and their thorough study by philatelists has resulted in the publication of several books, each devoted to a particular denomination of the series.[1] Collectors specializing in these issues will need to familiarize themselves with the information in these books, but a general collector can obtain a fairly good description of the various design types from any of the standard United States catalogs. Design alterations of these issues are most frequently encountered on the one, five, and ten-cent values, and some of the more common alterations are briefly discussed in the section on trimmed stamps in this chapter. However, due to the complexity of these issues, it would be wise to submit any copy offered as a scarce type to an acknowledged authority for examination.

---

[1]The reader is referred to this book's "Selected Bibliography" for the complete references to works by S. Ashbrook, C. Chase, H. Hill, and M. Neinken on the one-cent, three-cent, five-cent, and ten-cent stamps, respectively.

20th Century Issues

There are two twentieth century United States stamp designs which exist as a number of distinct types, and they are sometimes altered to defraud buyers.

The two-cent Washington Head design of 1908-1921 (Scott's Design No. A140) is divided by collectors into nine distinct types. Detailed descriptions of the minute differences in design are available from a number of sources.[2] These differences, while of major importance and worth careful study, are not the subject of this section. One type, however, is commonly altered. The faker attempts to change the common type III variety to the scarcer type II variety. Figures 4.1 and 4.2 illustrate and describe the major differences between the two types. Most often the type III stamp is altered to resemble the type II stamp by scraping one line of shading from each side of the ribbon. By inspecting the ribbon for any signs of scraping, and more importantly, by examining the other design characteristics as described, it can easily be determined if the stamp has been altered. Those stamps which can be so altered are summarized below:

Type III Stamp (Scott No.)	Corresponding Type II Stamp (Scott No.)
455	454
488	487
492	491
540	539

There are only two distinct design types of the two-cent Washington Head design of 1922-1932 (Scott's Design No. A157), the second type being much scarcer than the first. Four stamps are affected: two horizontal coils (Scott Nos. 599 and 599A), and two fully perforated stamps (Scott Nos. 634 and 634A). As with the previous two-cent design, there are several differences between the

[2]Johl, pp. 161, 169,175-7.

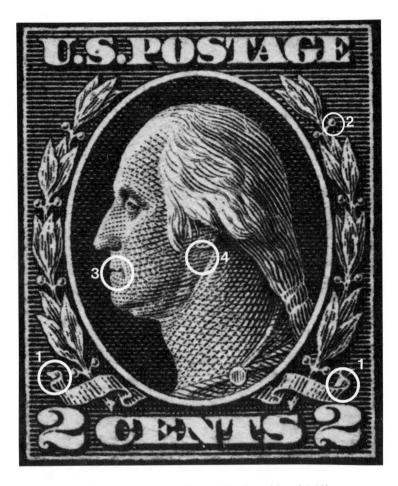

Figure 4.1. Type II Variety (Scott Design No. A140).

    1. There is a single line of shading in the top fold of the ribbon on the left, and in the second fold of the ribbon on the right.

    2. The top right laurel berry has a single shading dot.

    3. The dark line forming the mouth is straight across the bottom.

    4. There are several lines of shading below the ear which are severed.

Figure 4.2. Type III Variety (Scott Design No. A140).

1. There are two lines of shading in the top fold of the ribbon on the left, and in the second fold of the ribbon on the right.

2. The top right laurel berry has three shading dots which often run together to form a "V."

3. The dark line forming the mouth is crooked across the bottom, particularly at the end where it dips down.

4. The lines of shading below the ear are continuous, or nearly so.

63

Figure 4.3. Type I Variety (Scott Design No. A157).

1. There are no prominent hair lines at the top of Washington's wig.

2. There is a white line between the background and the wig at the back of Washington's head. The wig appears to "glow" in this area.

3. There is a thick line of color between the left oval and the frame line.

4. The four tiny circles in each corner are quite thick.

Figure 4.4. Type II Variety (Scott Design No. A157).

1. There are three prominent hair lines at the top of Washington's wig.

2. There is little or no white line between the background and the wig at the back of Washington's head.

3. There is a thin line of color between the left oval and the frame line.

4. The four tiny circles in each corner are quite thin.

two types, and they are illustrated and described in figures 4.3 and 4.4. The most commonly encountered fakes of the type II stamps are actually type I stamps in which the faker has strengthened the hair lines at the top of Washington's wig with an artist's brush. Therefore, it is important to be familiar with the other design differences. The appearance of the wig at the back of Washington's head is a feature which is difficult to successfully alter.

The color of the type II stamps is also an important consideration. Genuine type II stamps, whether they are the coil or the fully perforated variety, exist only in carmine-lake shades and never in bright carmine.

Perforated Issues Trimmed to Resemble Imperforate Issues

Fully perforated stamps can be trimmed on four sides, or trimmed to shape and then rebacked to resemble a corresponding, and presumably scarcer, imperforate issue. In addition to trimming the perforations, other changes are sometimes needed to complete the fake.

The 1851-1856 Issue

Fakes of this issue (Scott Nos. 5-17) can be made by trimming perforations from stamps of the perforated fifteen series of 1857-1861 (Scott Nos. 18-36). While it is theoretically possible to manufacture a large number of different fakes from this issue, the number commonly encountered is limited, as many of the perforated stamps are themselves quite valuable.

The rare, one-cent, type I imperforate stamp (Scott No. 5) can be faked by trimming the type I perforated stamp (Scott No. 18). However, the perforated stamp was not produced from the same plate as the imperforate, thus there are significant differences be-

66

tween the two. The perforated type I stamp has a secret mark consisting of a heavy shading dot in the white border surrounding the portrait oval at the left (fig. 4.5). In addition, genuine type I imperforates all show a slight double transfer in the top lettering and in the top right, side ornaments. The rarity of the type I imperforate stamp is such that any copy should be authenticated.

Figure 4.5. Secret Mark. Type I perforated stamps (Scott No. 18) differ from the imperforate stamp (Scott No. 5) in several ways, including the presence of a secret mark on the perforated stamp. Located in the white border surrounding the portrait oval at the left, it is one way to identify a perforated copy that has been trimmed to resemble the imperforate stamp.

By altering the design and trimming the perforations of the relatively common type V perforated stamp (Scott No. 24), fakes can be made to resemble any of the scarcer one-cent imperforates. These fakes can often be detected by a careful examination of the design and/or plating characteristics. However, scarce types that do not appear to be obvious fakes should be submitted to an authority for examination.

Trimmed fakes of the five-cent, red-brown, type I imperforate stamp (Scott No. 12) are most often made from the perforated stamp identical in color and design (Scott No. 28). There are also a number of fakes on record made from the brown, type I stamp (Scott No. 29); however, since the color is incorrect, detection is not difficult.

Trimmed fakes almost always have poor margins, as most perforated values from which the fakes are made have perforations that either touch or cut into the design. Thus, a faker will sometimes trim a perforated stamp to the exact shape of the stamp design and glue it to a new back with large margins. Often the original stamp is shaved or sanded down before being trimmed and glued to the new back, thus making it more difficult to detect the additional thickness. If necessary, design parts that may have been lost in the trimming process are painted in, and if the stamp is cancelled, parts of the cancellation are extended into the new margins. To detect such a fake, one should place the stamp face down in watermark fluid and observe the way the fluid is absorbed. Because of the glue used to attach the trimmed design, the body of this type of fake will usually absorb the fluid more slowly than the margins of the stamp. When completely saturated, the additional thickness in the design area will often result in this area appearing less translucent than the surrounding margins. Examination under ultraviolet light may also help to detect the added back or any design additions.

Fakes of the ten-cent values (Scott No. 13-16) are most commonly made from trimmed copies of the type V perforated stamp (Scott No. 35). This relatively common stamp exists with wide margins more often than any other value of the series, thus trimmed type V copies often appear to have the margins expected of the imperforates. However, the major difficulty in using this stamp to manufacture the imperforate varieties arises from the fact that it is a type V design, a type for which there is no corresponding imperforate issue. Therefore, the faker must also remove or add to parts of the design. Examination of the design with a good magnifying glass under both normal and ultraviolet light is therefore recommended.

Knowledge of the stamps' usual colors can also be helpful in detecting such fakes. Genuine imperforates are normally green or yellow-green, while those bogus imperforates made from the type V stamp are often blue-green.

The surest confirmation of such a fake, however, is to determine the plate position of the stamp in question. The ten-cent stamps have been successfully plated and this information is available in the literature.[3] At times the plating is made easier since fakers often attempt to manufacture the scarce and valuable type IV variety (Scott No. 16), a stamp that only occurs on eight readily identifiable plate positions.

Other Issues

The fully perforated five-cent 1902 issue (Scott No. 304) can be trimmed to resemble the scarcer imperforate variety (Scott No. 315). Only perforated copies with very large margins can even approximate an imperforate copy with acceptable margins. The color of the genuine imperforate is also important, it being a grayer blue than most perforated stamps. Sometimes seemingly imperforate copies will be offered for sale "as is." It is best to avoid these stamps and purchase instead a sheet margin copy, a multiple, or a single with unquestionably large margins. This recommendation holds true for any imperforate stamp. Imperforates of the one-cent value from the same series (Scott No. 314) and the two-cent shield design (Scott No. 320) can also be manufactured from the cor-

[3]Mortimer L. Neinken, *The United States Ten Cent Stamps of 1851–1859.*

responding perforated stamps (Scott Nos. 300 and 319, respectively). The imperforate four-cent value of this issue (Scott No. 314A) only exists with privately applied, type III Shermack perforations. It is a rare stamp, with less than fifty copies known, and as such should never be purchased without a certificate of authenticity.

The 1909 commemoratives all exist imperforate (Scott Nos. 368, 371, 373) and fakes are sometimes made by trimming the more common perforated stamps (Scott Nos. 367, 370, 372), or those with private vending machine perforations. Fakes produced by the former method are almost always too small, although the perforated Alaska-Yukon-Pacific Exposition Issue is known to commonly exist with wide margins. Trimmed private vending machine coils can result in presentable fakes. However, since many of these private coils are quite scarce, trimmed fakes are not too prevalent. Purchase these issues with wide margins, sheet margins, or in multiples.

Copies of the scarce, imperforate, rotary press coil of 1914 (Scott No. 459) can be manufactured by trimming copies of the corresponding perforated coil (Scott No. 453). Copies of #459 should only be purchased with ample margins at the left and right, or be purchased as a multiple. The colors of the two stamps are considerably different; #453 existing predominantly in shades of red, while #459 is most often found in shades of carmine.

Until recently, the rare, two-cent, type Ia imperforate issue (Scott No. 482A) was known only used, with type III Shermack perforations. A single unused copy without Shermack perforations is now known to exist. Fakes of this stamp can be made from the perforated type Ia stamp (Scott No. 500), but they are not common. The color and the impression of the two issues are different, the perforated stamp being more rosy and usually having a sharper impression than the imperforate.

The two-cent, type VII perforated stamp (Scott No. 528B) can be trimmed to resemble its corresponding imperforate issue (Scott No. 534B). The resulting fake, however, will more than likely have margins that are too small. A more convincing fake can be made by trimming a copy with type III Shermack perforations. The distance between the rows of these perforations is normally 20.0 mm plus or minus about 0.5 mm, and such private coils often measure exactly 25.0 mm high. Thus, imperforate copies of #534B that measure exactly 25.0 mm high and are narrower than 20.5 mm may well have been manufactured from the Shermack perforated stamp. Figure 4.6, while not a type VII stamp, is an example of the kind of fake imperforate that can be made from a type III Shermack coil. The

Figure 4.6. Trimmed Type III Shermack Coil Stamp. This seemingly imperforate stamp was manufactured from a copy with type III Shermack private perforations. It measures exactly 25 mm high and is 20.25 mm wide.

margins at the left and right are too small. Such stamps offered as imperforate issues should be avoided.

Table 4.1 is a summary of those United States issues which can be trimmed to resemble scarcer imperforate varieties. Though not a complete listing of all the possibilities, it lists those fakes which are most frequently encountered.

Table 4.1

Selected Fully Perforated United States Stamps that can be Trimmed to Resemble Imperforate Issues.

This Stamp Can Be Trimmed (Scott No.)	To Resemble This Stamp (Scott No.)
18	5
24	5–9
28,29	12
35	13–16
300	314
303	314A
304	315
319	320
319c	320b
319f	320a
367	368
370	371
372	373
453	459
500	482A
527	533
528B	534B
534B (Shermack ty. III)	534B

Proofs Altered to Resemble Issued Stamps

There are many plate proofs and some die proofs which are presently priced considerably lower than their corresponding stamps. Thus, a faker may at times attempt to manufacture a stamp from its proof.

Proofs are commonly printed on two types of paper. India paper is a soft, thin, opaque paper made from bamboo fiber, capable of showing the finest engraved impressions. Cardboard proofs are printed on a clear, white card stock which is considerably thicker than stamp paper. Both types of proofs, however, share the common characteristics of all proofs: the impressions are sharp and clear, and the colors are very bright.

Since India proofs are very thin, they must be rebacked if they are to resemble issued stamps. This is done simply by gluing an additional layer of paper to the back of the proof prior to any regumming or reperforating that may be required. The added layer can often be detected by placing the item in watermark fluid. As described earlier, the glue used to bind the new back to the proof often causes the fluid to be absorbed very slowly. Cardboard proofs must be sanded or shaved down if they are to approximate the thickness of stamp paper, and their absorption rate will often be comparable to issued stamps. However, as with any proof made to resemble an issued stamp, the impression will be too sharp and the color too bright. Additionally, one should always remember that any perforations and/or gum that may have been added will not have the characteristics of those found on genuinely issued stamps.

Removal of Manuscript Cancellations

The manuscript cancel, or pen cancel as it is sometimes known, enjoyed fairly wide use until shortly before the end of the nineteenth century. Since the permanence of many manuscript inks was poor, attempts are sometimes made to remove cancels applied in this manner. After the cancel has been removed, the stamp is often further cleaned to brighten its overall appearance. This procedure is usually followed by regumming. Stamps so treated will have a washed look. The stamp paper will appear abnormally bright. Extensive cleaning also tends to rough up slightly the surface of the paper, thus blurring an engraved impression. Examination under ultraviolet light will sometimes help to detect traces of the original cancel. Stamp paper that fluoresces a bright white under ultraviolet light has most likely been washed in some type of detergent. While this alteration can occur on any stamp, it is often encountered on the ten-cent issue of 1847 (Scott No. 2), the 1851-56 issue (Scott Nos. 5-17), and on high value bank note issues, particularly those for which there is a significant difference in the used and unused prices.

Color Alteration

Stamp colors can be altered by various chemical and physical treatments. While such alterations can at times result in dramatic color changes, they do not generally present any major problems in the field of United States philately. Very few U.S. stamps exist with color variations of significant value, and for those that do, the scarce colors cannot usually be manufactured very successfully by altering the cheaper color.

The four-cent Columbian blue color error (Scott No. 233a) is an exception, and fakes of this rarity are occasionally found. Recent studies using x-ray spectrometry have determined that the dye pigments in the blue error and the normal ultramarine stamp are very different chemically. The technique of false-color photography has also been successfully applied to the analysis of this stamp, and details of these methods are described in the literature.[4]

[4]R.H. White, editor, *Color in Philately* (New York, 1979).

Costly color varieties should be submitted for examination to competent authorities inasmuch as they can be difficult to identify without suitable reference material. While the changes of the color being faked are poor, there is always the possibility that the stamp in question is not the scarce color. Those United States stamps whose colors are difficult to correctly identify include the five-cent, red-orange stamp of 1847 (Scott No. 1c); the three-cent, orange-brown stamp of 1851 (Scott No. 10); the five-cent, brick-red and Indian-red stamps of 1858 (Scott Nos. 27, 28A); the three-cent, pink and pigeon blood-pink stamps of 1861 (Scott Nos. 64, 64a); the twenty-four cent, steel-blue stamp of 1861 (Scott No. 70 b); the four-cent Columbian blue error (Scott No. 233a); and the six-cent eagle airmail ultramarine error of 1938 (Scott No. C23c).

Exposure to sulphur compounds in the atmosphere can cause orange stamps to undergo a chemical change which results in their turning brown. The four-cent Trans-Mississippi issue (Scott No. 287) and the six-cent airpost issue of 1918 (Scott No. C1) are good examples of U.S. stamps which can be affected in this manner. The application of hydrogen peroxide will change the brown color to a colorless compound and thus the stamp will again appear orange.

The Addition of Guide-Lines and Joint-Lines to Coil Pairs

Flat plate printed coils normally exist with a guide line occurring every twenty stamps. These lines were engraved into the 400-subject plates used in the manufacture of these coils to help guide the perforators. Fakers sometimes paint fraudulent guide lines on plain pairs to make them resemble genuine guide line pairs. These added lines can almost always be detected by examining them with a good magnifier. Genuine guide lines are exactly the same color as the stamp; they are slightly raised, a characteristic of all engraved lines; the edges of the lines will be sharp; and there will be no trace of color inside the perforation holes, as often occurs when the lines are added.

The spacing between stamps is another feature to consider in determining the authenticity of guide lines on certain flat plate horizontal coils. In an attempt to improve poor centering caused by uneven paper shrinkage, 400-subject plates were prepared for some issues with the outer rows spaced three millimeters apart instead of the usual two millimeters. Since guide-line pairs come from a sheet's center rows, any guide-line pairs of Scott Nos. 352, 353, 387, 388, 394, and 395, which show three millimeter spacing are fraudulent. It should also be noted that Scott Nos. 392 and 393 were produced from plates with a uniform spacing of 2.75 mm, and therefore any pairs or guide-line pairs of these two issues showing only two millimeters spacing are bogus, having been made by re-perforating Scott Nos. 383 and 384.

When examining guide-line pairs, it should be kept in mind that the coil itself may be genuine, with only the guide line having been added, or it may be a totally manufactured pair, guide line and all.

Joint-line pairs are found only on rotary press printed stamps and result not from engraved guide lines, but from ink collecting in the crack where the two plates were joined after being curved to fit the rotary press cylinder. They normally occur every fifteen to seventeen stamps, depending upon the plate configuration. They are often far less regular in shape as compared to guide lines and can vary from a narrow, faint line to one that is heavy and dark. Fraudulent joint-lines are added and detected in exactly the same manner as that described for flat plate guide lines.

Counterfeit Overprints

Kansas-Nebraska Issue

Overprints are frequently the targets of counterfeiters, and this fact is easily explained. First, the overprints are often applied in a manner which makes them fairly easy to duplicate; and second, the overprinted stamp is often more valuable than the plain stamp. Fortunately for collectors of United States stamps, few issues have ever been overprinted. Of those that have, only the 1929 Kansas-Nebraska issues have been extensively counterfeited.

Issued in 1929, the Kansas-Nebraska overprints (Scott Nos. 658–679) were experimental stamps designed to thwart would-be robbers from stealing postage stamps in one state and selling them in another. The experiment was not successful, thus only the two series exist. Detailed descriptions of the production of these issues are available in the literature.[5]

The overprints were applied using electrotype plates after the stamps were printed, but before they were gummed. As a result, when viewed from the gum side, the overprints never appear impressed into the stamp, and any copy in which the overprint appears impressed is most likely counterfeit. Genuine Kansas and Nebraska overprints measure about 9.25 and 9.0 mm, respectively. Details of their spacing, serifs, and alignment can be seen in figures 4.7 and 4.8. Additional information on specific counterfeits is also available in the literature.[6]

While the intricacies of the overprint itself are important and deserve careful study, there are other features which can be helpful in detecting the majority of bogus copies in the marketplace today.

Color. Genuine Kansas-Nebraska overprints exist only on the 1929 shades of the perforated 10½ x 11 set, and in most values the differences in color are considerable when compared with other printings. These differences are of major importance when examining used copies and are summarized in table 4.2.

[5]Johl, pp. 304–307.

[6]Two articles appeared in the April, 1972 issue of the *American Philatelist,* "Counterfeit Kansas-Nebraska Overprints on 1922-23, 1923-26, 1926-34 Issues," compiled by Robert H. Schoen, and "The 'California Varieties' of Kans. and Nebr. Counterfeits," by Col. James T. DeVoss. They include detailed discussions of the many spacing and printing varieties, as well as descriptions of the known counterfeit overprints.

Figure 4.7. Genuine Kans. Overprints. Three slight variations of the genuine overprint.

Figure 4.8. Genuine Nebr. Overprints. Three slight variations of the genuine overprint.

Table 4.2

Colors of Genuine and Bogus
Kansas-Nebraska Stamps

Denomination	Color of Genuine Stamps	Color of Bogus Stamps
1c	Dull Yellow-Green	Blue-Green
1½c	Colors are Similar	
2c	Dark Dull Red	Bright Red
3c	Dark Dull Violet	Bright Violet, Red-Violet
4c	Dark Yellow-Brown	Light Yellow-Brown
5c	Dark Dull Blue	Light Blue
6c	Dull Orange	Bright Orange
7c	Grayish Black	Full Black
8c	Olive-Green	Olive-Bistre
9c	Dull Rose	Bright Rose, Orange-Red
10c	Colors are Similar	

Gum. In Chapter Two, details of gum breakers and ridged gum were discussed. Genuine Kansas-Nebraska stamps always have gum breakers that are 22 mm apart, thus most will show only one breaker, but occasionally two will be present, one at the very top and the other at the very bottom of the stamp. Kansas-Nebraska issues are also known for their ridged gum, and while not always a prominent feature, it will be evident in some degree on all genuine stamps.

Plate Numbers. Plate numbers used in the production of this series are listed in table 4.3.

Table 4.3

Plate Numbers Used in the Production of the Kansas/Nebraska Issue (Scott Nos. 658–679)*

Denomination	Kansas	Nebraska
1c	18957 19302, 19338, 19339	19338, 19339
1½c	19181, 19191	19182, 19192
2c	19174, 19175 19273 19379, 19383, 19384, 19385, 19398 19430, 19431, 19436, 19447	18989, 18990 19059 19204, 19205, 19233, 19378 19430, 19431
3c	18126 18803, 18804	18803, 18804
4c	18038, 18082	
5c	18907, 18908	
6c	18030, 18037	
7c	18736, 18740	
8c	18191, 18192	
9c	18742, 18744	
10c	19234, 19235	

*Source: *Durland Standard Plate Number Catalog.*

Hawaii Sesquicentennial Issue

Issued in 1928 (Scott Nos. 647–648), neither stamp is widely counterfeited, although of the two, the five-cent value is more often faked. The overprints were applied in the same manner as used for the Kansas-Nebraska issue, thus they will not appear to be im-

81

pressed when viewed from the gum side. Each genuine mint copy will have gum breakers spaced 22 mm apart and will show some degree of ridged gum. Since plate blocks command substantial premiums, they should be examined carefully. The plate numbers used in the production of these issues are as follows:

2c	18983, 18984
	19054, 19055
5c	18907, 18908

Bluish Paper Counterfeits

In 1909, the Bureau of Engraving and Printing, as a result of problems it was having with uneven paper shrinkage, began experiments with a paper containing 35% rag stock instead of the usual all wood pulp paper. The experiments were not successful, and today only eleven issues are known to be printed on this type of paper (Scott Nos. 357–366, 369).

Often collectors are surprised and perhaps somewhat disappointed after seeing a bluish paper issue for the first time. Most expect to see a much bluer stamp, while actually the color of the paper would be better described as pale bluish gray. Heavy inkings on some printings can mask the paper color so effectively that it is impossible to tell from the face side whether the stamp is a bluish paper variety.

One way to help see the bluish paper is to place the stamp or stamps in question face down on a large sheet of orange paper; the complementary color will help to accentuate any bluish color present in the stamp paper.

When held to a light, genuine bluish paper will appear to have a very fine, yet somewhat cloudy texture, whereas pulp paper will normally show a distinct mesh. Genuine bluish paper has numerous tiny, dark specks in the paper itself. Often the watermark when viewed by transmitted light will be well defined in bluish paper issues, a phenomenon not characteristic of ordinary paper. The position of the watermark is also important when examining these issues, and table 4.4 lists those positions recorded by W.S. Boggs.

Table 4.4

Positions of Bluish Paper Watermarks

Value	Scott No.	Watermark Position(s)
1c	357	Normal, Reversed, Inverted
2c	358	Reversed, Inverted
3c	359	Reversed, Inverted
4c	360	Reversed
5c	361	Normal, Inverted
6c	362	Normal, Reversed, Inverted
8c	363	Inverted
10c	364	Normal, Reversed
13c	365	Normal, Inverted
15c	366	Normal, Reversed, Inverted

Fake bluish papers are made by soaking a normal stamp in pale blue dye. Thus often the paper fibers at the ends of the perforation tips will show a stronger concentration of the dye. This feature can be accentuated by placing the stamp on the aforementioned orange paper.

Chapter Five

EXPERTIZING

Introduction

A philatelic item may be submitted for examination to a number or individuals, committees, societies, or foundations for inspection by acknowledged experts. For a fee, they will pass judgment on an item's authenticity and condition. They will then either sign the item or issue a certificate, usually with an attached photograph, stating their conclusions (fig. 5.1).

What Items Should be Submitted?

Stamps are generally submitted for two reasons. The first is to determine whether the stamp is genuine and has been correctly identified, and the second is to determine if the stamp has been altered, repaired, or damaged.

There are very few United States stamps that have been counterfeited. Most U.S. stamps are engraved, and as such they are not easily duplicated. While photographic techniques may result in copies that will pass through the mail undetected, a philatelist would not be fooled. However, those stamps printed by other methods such as typography, offset, and lithography can often be

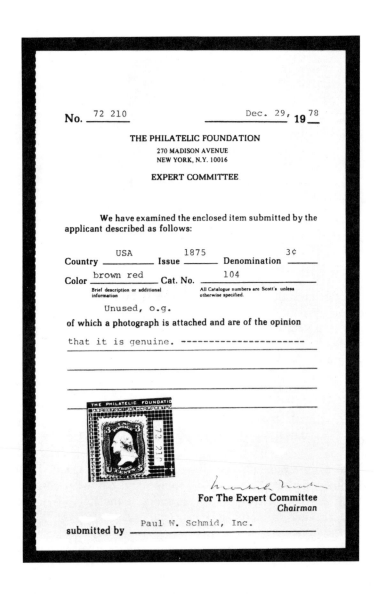

Figure 5.1 A typical photo-certificate issued by the Philatelic Foundation.

counterfeited quite successfully. Detection of such counterfeits can be difficult, and at times the only way to differentiate between the bogus and genuine is by direct comparison.

Often the problem facing an examiner is not one of trying to determine whether the stamp is genuine, but one of determining whether the stamp has been properly identified and cataloged. This problem exists for stamps of most countries. Subtle differences in color, gum, paper, grilling, or design will often result in completely different catalog listings and values. Some typical questions raised during the examination of United States stamps might be as follows:

> *Is the one-cent stamp of 1851 a design type III (Scott No. 8), or a type IIIa (Scott No. 8A)?*
>
> *Is the stamp a lightly grilled copy of the three-cent 1869 issue (Scott No. 114), a copy of the scarcer ungrilled variety (Scott No.114a), or is it the much rarer ungrilled reissue of 1875 (Scott No. 125)?*
>
> *Is the three-cent stamp of 1861 the rose-pink variety (Scott No. 64b), the scarcer pink variety (Scott No. 64), or the elusive pigeon blood pink variety (Scott No. 64a)?*
>
> *Is the eight-cent stamp of 1909 from the general issue (Scott No. 337), or an example of the rare bluish paper variety (Scott No. 363)?*

Differences in watermarks are usually easy to discern, but there are those stamps whose watermarks may present difficulties. For example, a stamp from the U.S. issue of 1914-15, with a single-line watermark barely visible at the corner, may easily be mistaken for the scarcer unwatermarked variety from the issue of 1916-17.

Proper identification, although difficult, is not the major problem facing expertizers today. Rather it is with altered and repaired stamps that the majority of problems exist. For here, the faker starts with a completely genuine stamp and alters or repairs it in such a way as to make it appear more valuable than it actually is. Typical examples of such alterations are:

The addition to or removal of an integral part of the design

The addition or removal of a surcharge or an overprint

The addition or removal of a grill

The addition or removal of perforations

The artificial color change of a stamp

There are many repairs that can be made on a stamp, and often they are done with considerable expertise. The addition of margins, filling of thins, or even the entire rebacking of a stamp are only some of the possibilities.

In trying to determine whether an item should be sent to an expertizing service, these questions must be answered:

Is the item of sufficient value to warrant the cost of the certificate?

Is the item one which is extensively counterfeited?

Will the saleability of the item be greatly enhanced if it has a certificate? For example, is the stamp one which can easily be confused with a cheaper variety?

Is there a reason to suspect that the item may be altered, repaired, or damaged?

Reconsiderations and Declined Opinions

All expert committees state that any conclusion they may reach regarding an item's authenticity is strictly an opinion. This opinion is subject to change and, in fact, at times it may be reversed. Just as an individual gains knowledge and experience over a period of years, so do expert committees, and an item is sometimes submitted for reconsideration. The opinions of an expert committee are based on a consensus of the examiners, and when individual opinions vary widely or are fairly evenly divided, the committee may choose to decline an opinion. Most sellers state in their terms of sale that a declined opinion is not grounds for the return of an item. The saleability of such an item, however, is jeopardized when an opinion is declined, and the buyer would be wise to try to find an acceptable committee or individual who will state an opinion.

Extensions

Reputable auction houses include a statement in their catalogs to the effect that all stamps are sold as genuine, and most give the buyer the opportunity to have the item expertized after it has been purchased. When the buyer chooses to do this, the item in question is said to be "on extension," and the auctioneer will hold the matter open until an opinion is rendered. Times and methods of notification, acceptable authorities, and other details may vary from dealer to dealer, and these terms should be carefully read prior to placing any bids. There are, however, some fairly consistent practices which deserve special mention:

1. The item in question must usually be paid for in full prior to the granting of an extension.

2. There is usually a time limit after which no refund will be made regardless of the opinion expressed. This term of sale should not be dismissed lightly in view of the fact that committees may take as long as six months to render an opinion.

3. A declined opinion by the examining committee is not sufficient reason for an item's return.

4. Costs for the entire expertizing procedure must be borne by the buyer if the item proves to be genuine. This seems a fair practice since the dealer originally sold the item as genuine in all respects. However, if the item is judged to be other than as described, the dealer will refund the purchase price and, within certain limits, pay for the cost of obtaining the opinion. It is within these limits that problems can arise. While by no means standard, an auction house will typically refund certificate costs up to 5% of the purchase price, but not exceeding $50. However, if one buys a stamp for $5000 and sends it to the Philatelic Foundation in New York, the certificate would currently cost in excess of $150 (including postage and handling). [1] Therefore, it would be wise to discuss such matters with the seller before making the purchase.

Buyers should also request an extension when purchasing stamps directly from a dealer. This amounts to no more than a request that the dealer refund the purchase price and certification costs should the stamp turn out not to be as represented. The dealer should be told of the intention to obtain such a certificate and agree to same at the time of the purchase. If the dealer is new to you, you may want the extension provisions in writing. If the dealer is one in whom you have confidence, then the extension procedure can be a

---

[1] In the case of the Philatelic Foundation, fees will be adjusted if the item is miscataloged by the submitter, found to be used instead of unused, or found to be counterfeit. The full fee is charged if the item is genuine but should happen to be reperforated, regummed, or repaired in any manner.

verbal agreement. If the dealer refuses to grant an extension, it is wise not to buy the stamp.

Altered and Bogus Certificates

Even though a stamp may have a certificate of some type, there still can be uncertainties regarding its authenticity, inasmuch as stamps with altered or bogus certificates have recently appeared in the marketplace.

An offer to sell a stamp with only a photocopy of the purportedly original certificate should be thoroughly investigated. Fakers have found it a relatively simple task to block out the original information on a certificate and substitute new data prior to making a photocopy. Sometimes all the original data as well as the photograph are changed, but more often than not, only a new photograph is substituted in place of the original. For example, the genuine certificate for a sound $4 Columbian stamp may be altered by placing a photograph of a different $4 Columbian, presumably one that is not sound, in place of the original photograph and then making a photocopy.

Some expertizing committees make their blank certificates available to anyone. The certificate is usually an integral part of the form used to submit an item for examination. It is relatively easy to obtain these forms, attach a photograph, and sign the certificate as genuine. Therefore, a careful examination of the raised seal which ties the photograph to the certificate should be made. Frequently this seal on genuine certificates is poorly impressed, and the faker takes full advantage of this fact, often using a totally unrelated corporate seal simply to give the bogus certificate the proper appearance.

The issuing committees will more than likely be quite willing to assist you with any inquiries you may have regarding a stamp's certificate, and they should be contacted if there is any reason to

91

believe that a certificate has been altered or faked.

Alteration After Certification

There can be a problem with a stamp that has an original photo-certificate, and it is directly related to the gum. Most certificates only state whether the stamp in question does or does not have original gum, making no reference to the hinging. The relatively recent demand by collectors for never-hinged stamps, and the subsequently high premiums for same, have given fakers a new opportunity to defraud buyers. Hinged stamps with good certificates that specifically mention original gum have become likely candidates for the fakers. They simply remove the hinged original gum, regum the stamp, and then offer it as never-hinged, with what will appear to be a perfectly legitimate certificate to substantiate their claim.

There are two ways to combat this problem. The first is to simply submit the item for re-examination, preferably to the same committee. A second approach would be to contact the issuing committee and request that they check their files. Very often the work sheets that some committees keep on each item they have examined will have notations regarding the hinging. If there is a difference between the present state of the gum and what is noted on the work sheet, the stamp must be resubmitted. Since there will be additional fees incurred, these procedures should be used only when, after careful examination, regumming is suspected.

Signed Stamps

When a recognized authority examines a stamp and then places his name or initials on the back, using either a tiny rubber stamp or simply by writing with a pencil, the stamp is said to be "signed" (fig. 5.2). Auction catalogs will often include the notation, "signed _____."

Figure 5.2 Signed Stamps. The example on the left has a hand-stamped signature, while that on the right is signed by hand in pencil.

Since a stamp is generally signed in lieu of a photo-certificate, caution should be exercised when purchasing such a stamp. Signed stamps are not always genuine, as signatures can be easily faked.

After buying a collection, a dealer will often request an expert to examine and sign the rare and often-faked items. This procedure saves the dealer time and expense. Those items that are pronounced genuine can be sold privately or at auction with excellent assurance that any item carried on extension will come back genuine. The relatively quick examination by the signer will also allow the dealer time to work out a satisfactory arrangement with the seller regarding those items which are judged to be fake.

Collectors who follow a similar procedure can often obtain the same benefits. This is not to suggest, however, that collectors should not get photo-certificates for valuable stamps, but simply to inform collectors of the alternatives. One point should be evident: a signed stamp is of real value only to the individual who had it signed. It gives the individual some assurance that when the stamp is resold, there will most likely be no problems should the new buyer want to get a photo-certificate. Purchasing an expensive stamp that is only signed, and then forgetting about it until the time comes to sell is, at the very least, risky. Either have the signature confirmed by the signer, have it signed by someone new, or get a photo-certificate. The decision should be based on cost, time, saleability, and the buyer's own peace of mind.

Be aware of the fact that signatures on never-hinged stamps can sometimes result in a decreased value for the stamp. Some buyers willing to pay substantial premiums for never-hinged material feel that a signature defaces the gum. This concern is particularly applicable though not limited to twentieth century European stamps.

Expertizing Services

The following are a few of the foundations, societies, and committees that offer expertizing services:

American Philatelic Society Expertization Committee
P.O. Box 8000
State College, PA 16803
Phone: 814-237-3803
World-Wide Issues

The Philatelic Foundation
501 5th Ave. Room 1901
New York, NY 10017
Phone: 212-867-3699
World-Wide Issues

Royal Philatelic Society
41 Devonshire Place
London W1, England
British Area

British Philatelic Association
446 Strand
London WC 2R ORA, England
British Area

American First Day Cover Society Expert Committee
Allison W. Cusick
P.O. Box 141379
Columbus, OH 43214
First Day Covers

It may be the policy of some expertizing groups to indelibly mark stamps they believe to be bogus. By applying words such as "false" or "counterfeit" to the stamp, they effectively remove it from the marketplace. Notwithstanding the ethical questions which result from such a practice, this procedure can create an immediate practical problem. Many auction houses state they will accept a return only if the stamp is in the same condition as originally purchased. It would, therefore, be wise for the buyer to check with the dealer regarding acceptable authorities before submitting any item for expertizing. Direct inquiries to expertizing groups regarding their policies are also recommended.

SELECTED BIBLIOGRAPHY

Ashbrook, Stanley B. *The United States One Cent Stamp of 1851 - 1857.* 2 volumes. New York: H.L. Lindquist, 1938.

Boggs, Winthrop S. *The Foundations of Philately.* New York: The Philatelic Foundation, 1955.

Brookman, Lester G. *The 19th Century Postage Stamps of the United States.* 3 volumes. New York: H.L. Linquist, 1966.

Chase, Carroll. *The 3c Stamp of the United States 1851 - 1857 Issue.* Springfield, MA: Tatham Stamp & Coin Company, 1942.

DeVoss, James T. "The 'California Varieties' of Kans. and Nebr. Counterfeits." *American Philatelist,* 86: 310-312 (April, 1972).

Durland Standard Plate Number Catalog. Boston: Sterling Stamp Co., Inc., 1979.

Fellows, Robert. "Postage Stamp Restoration." *Stamps* (April 7, 1973), pp. 14 - 24.

Fellows, Robert. "Postage Stamp Restoration." *Stamps* (April 14, 1973), pp. 82 - 88.

Hill, Henry W. *The United States Five Cent Stamps of 1851 - 1861.* Henry W. Hill, 1955.

Howard, George P. *The Stamp Machines and Coiled Stamps.* New York: H.L. Lindquist, 1943.

Johl, Max G. *United States Postage Stamps 1902 - 1935.* Lawrence, MA: Quarterman Publications, Inc., 1976.

Neinken, Mortimer L. *The United States One Cent Stamp of 1851 to 1861.* U.S. Philatelic Classics Society, Inc., 1972.

Neinken, Mortimer L. *The United States Ten Cent Stamps of 1851 - 1859.* Mortimer L. Neinken, 1960.

Schoen, Robert H. "Counterfeit Kansas - Nebraska Overprints on 1922 - 23, 1923 - 26, 1926 - 34 Issue." *American Philatelist,* 86: 303-310 (April, 1972).

Scott Specialized Catalogue of United States Stamps 1979. New York: Scott Publishing Co., 1978.

White, R.H., editor. *Color in Philately.* New York: The Philatelic Foundation, 1979.

Williams, L.N. and M. *Fundamentals of Philately.* State College, PA: American Philatelic Society, Inc., 1971.

INDEX BY SCOTT NUMBER

SUBJECT INDEX

Gum creases, cause of, 16-7; appearance of, 17-8

Gum disturbances, 21-6

Gum soaks, 25

Gum skips, 18

Guide lines, addition of fake, 75-6

Hill, Henry W., 60

Hinges, used to conceal thin, 4; removal of, 24-5

Hinging, definitions of, 23

Included perforations, 10-11

Inclusions. *See* Included perforations. *See* Paper specks

Johl, Max G., 49, 61, 77

Joint-Lines, addition of fake 75-6

Kansas/Nebraska issue, *See* Overprints, Kansas/Nebraska issue

Margins, added, 14, 68, 88

Neinken, Mortimer L., 60, 69

Original gum, thins in stamps with, 3; affect on stamp price, 15; on flat plate stamps, 16-9; on rotary press stamps, 19-22; regumming with same formula as, 28

Overprints, Hawaii Sesquicentennial issue, 81-2

Overprints, Kansas/Nebraska issue, color of genuine stamps, 77, 80; appearance of genuine, 78, 79; gum on, 80; plate numbers used, 80-1

Page remnants, 25-6

Paper specks, 11

Perforation, rotary, 32-4, 36, 38-40, 43; characteristics of genuine holes produced by, 38-40

Perforation, stroke, 31-2, 38

Perforations, short or missing, 8-9; separated, 9-10; rejoined, 10; included, 10-11

Perforation hole, definition of gauge of, 37; correct size of, 37-8, 41, 54; appearance of genuine, 38-40, 41-2, 43, 45-7; appearance of bogus, 39-40

Perforation tips, appearance of genuine and bogus, 42-3

Philatelic Foundation, 86, 90, 95

Pinholes, 10

Plate blocks, separated perforations in, 9-10

Proofs, characteristics of fakes manufactured from, 72

Rebacking, definition of, 13; detection of, 13-4; examples of, 73, 88

Regummed stamps, reasons for, 27; detection of, 27-9

Repairs. *See individual listings*

Reperforation, definition of, 34-5; reasons for, 35; use of gauges in determining,